Acclaim for

Dawn Songs

"Reaser and Lanham have brought together a cornucopia of talent to celebrate the lives of birds in *Dawn Songs*. Each piece in the collection extols the lives of feathered travelers, from falcon and swift to murre and warbler, simultaneously imparting rich tidbits of life history and the joys of being an observer. This new twist to a field guide makes learning about birds a lyrical adventure."
– Susan Bonfield, Environment for the Americas

"*Dawn Songs* is unlike any bird book that I have ever encountered. In addition to challenging us to learn about the habits and behaviors of migratory birds, the Reader's Guide explicitly invites us to study the human animal – to be keen self-observers! How? By cultivating attentiveness, patience, curiosity, and wonderment with the other-than-human world. Nature is inclusive of human nature. YES ... We are all kindred spirits."
– Christopher Uhl, Penn State University, author of *Awaken 101*

"Lyrical, mesmerizing and inspiring; these words apply equally to birds in all their globe-circling glory, and to the luminous works of prose and poetry in *Dawn Songs* that celebrate migratory birds, that agitate and advocate and sometimes mourn on their behalf, and which open our hearts and ears to their majesty and beauty."
– Scott Weidensaul, author of *A World on the Wing*

"Too often we forget to simply celebrate the natural world. I didn't know I needed a poetry collection about bird migration, but it turns out the beauty and wonder captured by the poets featured in *Dawn Songs* were exactly what my soul was longing for."
– David Mizejewski, National Wildlife Federation

"The poems and short essays in *Dawn Songs* affect us the way birds do: They lift our spirits, they make us sad, they rekindle memories, and in doing so, they make us more aware of our own lives and the lives of others (human and non-human). *Dawn Songs* also makes us care more about a natural world that is so essential, so resilient, and yet so vulnerable."
– David S. Wilcove, author of *No Way Home: The Decline of the World's Great Animal Migrations*

Dawn Songs

A Birdwatcher's Field Guide
to the Poetics of Migration

Jamie K. Reaser
J. Drew Lanham
editors

TALKING WATERS PRESS · *Schuyler, Virginia*

Cover and text design by Jason Kirkey
Cover art © Mark Collins

ISBN: 978-0-9968519-4-7
First Edition 2023
Talking Waters Press
Schuyler, Virginia

...Oh let us be
a bird flying wholly for the sake
of flying, to be that breath-
machine that even the anchored
earth-bound wavers want
to root for, want to look up
and say, rally, rally, win.

— FROM DRIFT BY ADA LIMÓN

Contents

TO LAMENT

DAWN SONGS

THE WINTERING GROUNDS

Jamie K. Reaser

Our field site was nestled in the jungle, about a mile down an old logging road, at a turn in the Rio Bravo River, beneath a canopy of tall, deciduous hardwoods – white gombolimbo, hog plum, bastard mahogany, and royal palm to name a few. It was termed a primitive camp – our tents and personal gear, a fire pit surrounded by stumps on which we sat, a tarp over a make-shift kitchen, a latrine dug lengthwise behind a fallen tree. Mosquitoes, mud, bellowing howler monkeys, and things that went bump in the blackness of night could be encountered in this place, in that particular order.

We were there for the birds – mostly, the Neotropical migratory birds – the small songbirds that had flown from somewhere far north of Belize to this particular forest, termed secondary palm and broadleaf in composition. These passerines were our subject of study under the auspices of the Manomet Bird Observatory (now, simply known as Manomet). We had come to meet them on their wintering grounds, where they make up about 25% of the avian fauna.

We brought questions with us: What migrants are here? What parts of the forest do they inhabit? What do they eat? Who eats them? Do they form mixed-species foraging flocks? If so, with whom? What are their interactions with the resident birds – is there resource competition, cooperation?

We set up mist nets so that we could take birds in hand. To do so necessitated that we swing machetes to widen tapir trails. We cut away palms and cut down bamboo to serve as poles that we'd pound into the riparian muck. The long nets were strung in between. When we caught an unwitting migrant – one that had been unable to see the fine black mesh of the net while navigating the dense, lowland scrub – we clamped an individually numbered metal band on its leg – left for female and right for male. This would enable anyone who found the bird, anywhere, to contact the U.S. Geological Survey's Bird Banding Lab in Patuxent, Maryland to report the finding and learn about the bird's banding history. Banding is one of the ways that scientists learn where, when, and how migrants migrate.

Red-eyed vireo. Gray catbird. Magnolia warbler. Northern waterthrush. Hooded warbler. American redstart. Black-and-white warbler. Willow flycatcher. Gray-cheeked thrush. Swainson's thrush.

We demarcated visual and vocal encounter survey routes – paths that we walked in a standardized manner, at a particular pace, with specific stopping points where we'd pause for just so long to look and listen and write down our observations. Who did we see? Who did we hear? Some nights, we surveyed by playing recordings of various tropical owl calls. You could count on an answer from the spectacled owl that kept close to camp – a deep, knocking and PUP-pup-pup-pup-po, POK pok pok bog bog bog boboboo. And too, there were the trills of one or both of a pair of vermiculated screeches. They and the bats worked the old logging road airways from dusk 'til dawn, the katydids stridulating all the while at the flanking forest edge.

We mapped vegetation structure and plant type so we could

correspond habitat to bird use of the habitat. In the tropics, you need be quite wary of thorns and saps. They will tear your clothes, puncture your skin, burn you, and invite nasty infections. You need to watch where you put your hands while being mindful not to step on a fer de lance or in an ant mound.

We also set up a few focused studies. For example, in addition to the metal anklets, some birds received unique combinations of colored, plastic bands so we could follow individuals around and document their activities. I wanted to know how the birds stratified use of the forest – from leaf litter floor to canopy top – so teamed up to devise and launch a four-tiered panel of mist nets that unfolded as they were hoisted and folded again when dropped on a pully system. Would the same bird species be routinely caught at the same height? Another team focused on red-capped manakins – a short, stout, iridescently plumed resident bird. The male sports yellow trousers, black body, and red head, while the female is olive green above and dusty-yellow below. The question was, "What makes a male manakin a highly preferable erotic dancer?" That's right: the males spend the day in groups, known as leks, performing various displays – branch to branch slides, jigs, twists, leaps, shimmies, scuffles, and flights while snapping their wings to click and clack and explosively pop – in the hope of being selected by a female for seasonal copulation. That's right: it's ladies' choice. She shows up to see what savvy moves the gents have to offer.

At the time we did this work, in early 1991, the decline of Neotropical migratory bird populations was just beginning to garner priority attention from conservation scientists, land managers, and policy makers. I had heard the alarm call a year earlier, as I began the final semester of my senior year in college. Loud and clear, it came through John Terborgh's newly released, *Where Have All the Birds Gone?* For some species, habitat loss, habitat fragmentation, and predation by domestic cats were obvious problems on their breeding grounds in the United States and Canada. But the declines of other migratory species could not be so readily discerned – you had to wonder what was happening on the wintering grounds. What was happening while these birds inhabited Central or South America, or the Caribbean?

To answer this question, the ornithologists who enjoyed the company of Neotropical migrants during the northern summer months had to get up and go. We had to board planes and flock in our own way to the wintering grounds.

We had to show up for the birds.

※

What does it mean to show up for another – where they are at?

Several years ago, I was in a workshop in Portland, Oregon, facilitated by don Américo Yábar, a Peruvian of Basque bloodline who grew up in the Andes among the Q'ero – indigenous descendants of the Inca – peoples who live at high elevation, largely on corn, potatoes, coca leaves, and prayer to the spirits that imbue everything: every thing, a being. I'd known Américo for fifteen years or so at that point. We'd travelled into the Andes together, and to the shores of Lake Titicaca. Sat in ceremony with the Q'ero together. Shared poetry together.

Américo is the founder of the poetic S'alka Movement – a contemplative practice based on Q'ero cosmology that brings heart to mind at the interface of Nature and human nature. He translates the Quechua word "s'alka" as undomesticated energy. Simply put, to engage in the poetics of s'alka is to show up as freed as possible from the sharply-focused constructs of the linear-rational Western mind. It is to see literally, metaphorically, and metaphysically with a soft gaze. As a scientist who writes poetry, I'm a curiosity to don Américo. "Mirada suave," he often teased when people asked me to identify plants and animals or discuss scientific matters during our trips. "Mirada suave," he'd grin and shake his head, looking askance at me. Soft gaze.

I'd gone to Portland to surprise him. Tears welled in his eyes when he turned and saw me. "Anyi" is sacred reciprocity. Tears can be anyi, when one fully shows up for another.

We, a group of us, were sitting on felled logs in a sun-filtered woodlot behind a community center. Don Américo asked us to pair up for an exercise, choosing new partners. During the previous exercises that morning I'd noticed that one of the women had been self-marginalizing – sitting off to the side and physically leaning away from the group, head down. There was an empty log in front of her. I approached. "May I join you where you are at?" I inquired. Her head rose. Her eyes watered. She glanced at me, her body softening, and she nodded.

After the exercise she shared my question with the group:
"May I join you where you are at?"
She'd never been asked such a question before.
It's a poetically s'alka question when asked with a soft gaze.
"May I join you where you are at?"
The group fell silent.
Américo looked at me – looked into me – and smiled.
It's a simple question, or is it?

What makes it so challenging for us to see where another person is at and show up for them there – to meet another person on the ground they occupy – physically, in their state of mind, and in their belief systems?

Would it be easier if we remembered that we *Homo sapiens* are animal? King Philip came over from German soil.

Kingdom:	Animalia
Phylum:	Chordata
Class:	Mammalia
Order:	Primates
Family:	Hominidae
Genus:	*Homo*
Species:	*sapiens*

That's how I learned it anyway.
Some answers you can find in books. Some you can't.
Scientists tend to have large personal libraries. Book cases are

filled and stacked upon as if the answers to all the big questions reside there and somehow will enter us – by some sort of osmosis, perhaps – even if the books aren't read. And, they won't be. Most of them anyway, if we scientists are truthful about it.

Over the years, I've begun to restrain this habit, donating books to libraries and passing them on to colleagues who will someday burden their long-dreading children with the voluminous literary acquisitions of scientific merit.

Among what I have kept, there are old, musty, jacketless hardbacks that tell stories – stories about animals and the places they inhabit. They are stories held within my bloodline, often as gifts given and received. There is longing, searching, rawness, and vulnerability inherent in these works. There is a pattern of showing up, in the hope of finding – or being found.

My great grandfather, John Earl Carpenter – Papa – was an avid outdoorsman. I have black and white photos of him in a fishing camp. Enormous watermelons, each with a whiskey bottle on top, sit at the entrance to a large group tent, where he lounges with men and women unknown to me.

Papa's personal library bookplate, his *Ex Libris*, resides in John J. Rowlands' *Cache Lake Country: Life in the Northwoods* (1947), Wyman Richardson's *The House on Nauset Marsh* (1955), David B. Ericson's and Goesta Wollin's *The Ever-Changing Sea* (1967), and his blue ballpoint signature claims Will O. Douglas' *My Wilderness: East to Katadin* (1961) and Sigurd F. Olson's *The Lonely Land* (1961).

One of the many things that I find fascinating about books is that they can bring a singular narrative to so many people, across generations. Papa was an elderly man when these books were published and I had not yet come into the world. Yet – decades apart – the same words arising from the same voices spoke to us about the intimacy of place, the kinship of flora and fauna:

"I knew then I had found the place I had always wanted to be." – J.J. Rowland

"And you should hear the soft warble of a bluebird, you may imagine him encouraging his trusting group of smaller bethren and guiding them to their destination. The thought of this relationship has somehow given me great comfort. Through the dark passages that must sometimes be negotiated, what better guide could one have than the cheerful, sagacious robin or the unpretentious, care-taking, sensible bluebird?" – W. Richardon

"Naturally, we land dwellers know about and take a greater interest in the part of the earth that lies above sea level. Our planet is the only sample of the universe with which we can become familiar; but the oceans cover three quarters of that sample. To attain the fullest possible awareness and understanding of our little speck of the universe we shall have to turn more and more to the study of the oceans." – D. B. Ericson and G. Wollin

"In the flood plains where the sweet gum, elm, and red maple flourish, I found red-bellied woodpeckers, scarlet tanagers, red-shouldered hawks, and Kentucky warblers. Where the oaks and tulip trees grow, I kept company with cardinals, Carolina wrens, broad-winged hawks, and yellow-throated vireos." – W. O. Douglas

"The sunset was a gorgeous one – flaming streams of color against the last wisp of clouds. Ducks whispered overhead, and the air was alive with the sound of the rapids below." – S. F. Olson

I have Papa's silver-tipped bamboo fly rod. It's tucked away for safe keeping, somewhere.

My grandmother was born Helen Howell Carpenter. For Christmas, in 1953, my grandfather, William E. Reaser, gave her Olson's *Listening Point*. He addressed it to Peg. He signed it Bill.

"Over toward the far point where the lone pine stood, I heard a faint splash and saw a spout of silver as a beaver slapped its tail and dove, and then I followed the wake of its swimming far toward the open, watched until I merged with the sunlit ripples and was gone." – S. F. Olson

It was my grandmother who taught me to fish, on a little dock on the side of Carnegie Lake where large, brazen carp spun about and small woeful bluegills puckered and nabbed the misfortunate worms that I'd plucked from dark, damp topsoil earlier that morning, wriggling as best they could – trying their best to stay where they had been living their subterranean lives in the back corner of my grandparents' yard, at the edge of long-molding leaf piles and thick beds of pathologically trimmed *Pachysandra*.

On Easter in 1967, Papa gifted my parents Roger Tory Peterson's *A Field Guide to the Birds* (1947) and George A. Petrides' *A Field Guide to Trees and Shrubs* (1958). In 1967, Easter fell on Sunday, March 26th. On December 13, 1967 – about nine months later – I showed up.

They didn't stay long – these ancestors who inhabited books about the natural world. At 55, I've now lived more of my life without them than with them.

It's an odd thing to hold these memoirs and novels, to turn their thick, yellowed pages and think that these particular stories – these stories so full of attentiveness, of curiosity, of devotion, of gratitude – are my inheritance. It is simultaneously soothing and befuddling, satisfying and evocative – evocative in that it evokes a sense of emptiness, and a longing to fill that void that is too far down the bloodline for me to reach with names.

What I have sought after and found in Nature was not present in familial human nature. At least, not in the way I knew human nature to be during those years in which there was family. With very little exception – like when fishing, perhaps – there wasn't eager togetherness. There wasn't wonderment about the human landscape that was us and in which we collectively dwelled. There wasn't tenderness, nor joy in the observation of another.

There was a bushel basket of balls and a badminton set in my grandparent's closet – in the bottom right far corner – that were pulled out and placed in the yard on the rare occasion that the grandchildren were brought to visit. Said grandchildren were to remain outside to the fullest extent of the day possible, playing quietly. When indoors, we were to be seated at card tables, playing Go Fish and King in the Corner at a whisper. Slap Jack was prohibited. We could watch TV when a baseball game was on, but only if we sat on the floor in silence. At the dinner table too there was to be silence but for two exceptions: 1) the giving of the blessing and 2) recitation from the dictionary that lived in the middle of the dining room table. "Eleemosynary. Noun. Charitable. My mother works for an eleemosynary institution." There are lessons you don't forget.

But, when I think of my last attempted visit with my grandfather, it's not the dreaded silence but screaming that I recall – I hear him bellowing and screeching to the nurses in the infirmary to remove his grandchildren from his room, seconds after we'd entered it. His entire body, bound into a hospital chair, was shaking. To him, our presence was worse than the electroshock therapy he'd endured for years. He couldn't have understood the reason we had arrived there at that time, nor what it foretold. In another part of the building his wife of over fifty years was dying of a brain tumor. His youngest of two daughters, my mother, was terminally ill with breast cancer. He'd be gone within the year from undiagnosed causes. It was considered a blessing.

In my family system there was a relational hardness and a stark chill, like what was once verdant had become frozen. And remained frozen. It was a frozen land.

I was born in winter. I was born into that winter.

I believe that people can return from the wintering grounds. Animals will depart the grounds of scarcity when abundance becomes available to them elsewhere.

"May I join you where you are at?"

Upon my return from Belize, I joined Russ Greenberg in creating the Smithsonian Migratory Bird Center, a research and education program focused on Neotropical migratory birds and their conservation across the Western Hemisphere. Our book, *Bring Back the Birds: What You Can Do to Save Threatened Species*, was intended to complement Terborgh's call to action – it provided concerned citizens with guidance on a wide range of actions that could be taken for the birds.

But in all the worrying and finger pointing and what-to-dos about the birds, I felt there was something missing. We were missing the stories about these animals and the places they inhabit – stories told in such a way as to invoke human longing, searching, rawness, and vulnerability. We needed to celebrate these migrants and the migratory phenomenon. We needed to acknowledge the relief we feel when these birds return declaring winter's end, to claim the joy of the ensuing dawn chorus.

Thus, in 1993, the Smithsonian Migratory Bird Center joined with Partners in Flight-Aves de las Americas to launch International Migratory Bird Day on the second Saturday in May across the Western Hemisphere. It was intended to be a celebration. We wanted people to pick up a pair of binoculars or a spotting scope and go look for birds, to go learn about birds, to do something for the birds in a way that was fun and mattered – and was done together.

We wanted people to show up where the birds are at.

Thirty years later, under the banner of World Migratory Bird Day, they still are. People are still showing up for the birds. And, I pray – knowingly or not – for each other.

People can return from the wintering grounds.

IDENTITY

J. Drew Lanham

I have spent the balance of my life years identifying birds – naming them by wing bars and whistled call; by character of tail wags and parsing bill shape by primary plumage color or preference for Montana tall grass prairie or Lowcountry South Carolina pluff mud and salt marsh. From the most subtle shading of a feather to the most obvious flashing of vermillion, I have come to know the difference between long-billed curlews and whimbrels, between Henslow's sparrow and painted buntings. I have been drawn into mixed flocks of blackbirds that many people would just as soon dismiss of diversity and lump into one – one black bird.

It has been a satisfying journey of discovery to learn birds as fellow Earth travelers. It allows for a persistent striving to push beyond surviving, to thriving. After all, whether winged or not, we share the same air, same water, same soil. We are in common plight, the birds and us. Our ranges – literal and metaphoric –

overlap. And so, a great part of the bird-labeling quest has led me to want to be a part somehow of solutions that push my selfish love beyond watching and into more selfless action – to save and conserve. To love even harder still, yes, but to imbue that affection with some action that restores or makes better what is – or has been. To be intentionally intense in some way bent towards wildness and wild things so that what is left behind us is not in ruins but great reward for those yet to come.

In my migration from a bird-loving country boy to a professional ornithologist to the activist conservationist creative writer I am now, I have come to realize that as I was coming into this understanding of what birds are, I was also coming into a deeper understanding of who I am. My journey with birds has inspired me into my own being.

MIGRATION

what thoughts ramble
in the redstart's brain
as the day draws closed
as dusk descends?
is it larval fuel to lay on fat?
a steady southbound wind?
perhaps it's the flicker
of unseen light
the lure of tropical terrain
is it the flight plan hard-wired –
instinct etched in
by design not likely to change?
or does some warbler learned Plan B
come into play
by circumstance rearrange?
fare thee well little bird
may stars bright guide you true
to thicket lush
past falcon's rush

through dark skies inky blue
it's my hope
that neither cat
nor glass
will spell your odyssey's end
but that your tiny wings
some luck
some skill
will bring you back
to inspire me once again

I am best when I am out and about and among the wild birds and beasts and places where my thoughts flow fastest – one moment as rushing mountain river rapids and then, next, slow to slack flowing like the same water receding from blackwater cypress swamp. My mission to conserve the wild has enabled me to explore, delineate, define, map, and navigate the varied landscape that is humanity – that is me. I may migrate away from myself, but I always return.

The plight of wild birds has called me to teach – to teach as an act of inquiry. I am not so interested in instilling immutable facts as I am inspiring thinking that might someday lead to wider caring and conserving acts. To inquire and find out what and how – and then to inquire again to, perhaps, open the doors to why. That has been my life. That is my life.

Now, words mean something more to me than the statistical significance. As a writer-teacher, I am able to share by prose and verse an abiding love for our beloved birds and the wildness they inhabit and convey unto us. This has been the greatest of life-emergent gifts – it is seeing a bird and knowing it is more than its Latin binomial or common name can express. Its technical identity matters less than its being. Our human identities – our individuality in the collective of *Homo sapiens* – matter in various ways, often by who others see us as, but most importantly by how we see ourselves.

To be able to connect the dots – to bring culture and conservation together in the inclusive convergence that, hopefully, broadens our scope of understanding and impact. To nurture and protect and do better, so better is possible going beyond us. To have everyone know that our responsibility lies in care. That, quite simply and profoundly, is conservation. Art and science – when linked in common cause – can motivate this stewardship.

Charley Harper's art is symbolic of this linkage and emblematic of the avian beauty and diversity we must work to protect, by poetry and prose, by practice and policy. Look it up. There is a simplicity to Harper's work that forwards identification *of* a particular species or habitat or behavior into identification *with* it. In his painting, *Mystery of the Missing Migrants*, a mixed flock of migratory birds plies the star-studded night skies bound elsewhere. North or south, we cannot say. Harper's genius minimalist technique leaves no doubt as to "what" something is. The totality of his work guides me to want to "feel" more than know. His migratory mystery reflects all we know, but even more of what we don't now – perhaps, the unknowable. Crucial in this patchwork quilt of feathered beings is the impression – the gestalt – of a "united" effort of diverse individuals moving towards some common goal.

ZUGUNRUHE ON CANVAS

A flock of geometry
A transgulf journey of bird-adoring minimalism
cast against
a midnight blue black sky pin-pricked
by mustard yellow dot stars.
A palm tree in silhouette shadowed below
the still-life gathering moving.
The roll call made easy;
golden-cheeked, prothonotary, cerulean, blackpoll,
bay-breasted, Cape May,
Blackburnian, black-throated gray,
Townsend's, redstart, hooded,

chestnut-sided, parula warblers accounted for.
The scene is urgent at the edge of my dreams
scarlet tanager. black-throated green warbler
swallow-tailed kite staring back through the canvas as if to ask
"who me?"
Swainson's thrush with buffy-ness enough to tell
what it is.
A yellow-billed cuckoo a foot long –
my grandmother's rain crow,
caught by pastel oils in sudden turn.
A decision to go here and not there?
To settle on lower Mississippi River delta to eat
camp caterpillars
instead of calling storms further east and north?
perhaps.
Gestalt is a Feel, given just a hint
A glimpse of possibility by pieces of plumage,
nothing more.
A triangle as Bill or body
arcs and semicircles for wings.
All glimpse enough to tell
this one migratory being from that other
peregrinating sojourner.
But each nuanced to be more
and then less
Tail splayed to stop
or straight out to jet by
depending on
climb or dive or direct neotropics
to temperate ground route.
The mass of hues reduced to shapes.
Unlike anything John James
would have killed, posed, painted –
then ate.
Whimsy as artful intent.

To make life emerge from print
with imagination flowed from palette to brush.
The flock forever in head sparked to heart.
A box of 64 colors made into something greater
than between the lines coloring would render.
But then –
beyond those mysterious migrants
missing more and more from dawn landed chorus,
Charley did more with less.
Reduced biodiverse detail to make ID obvious.
And in the creating no birds died.
No graves were robbed
skulls fondled or
Black people enslaved in the process.
I marvel
at a quetzal perched mid-canopy
in the midst of a few lush greens
to make us know Costa Rican cloud forest.
A bobwhite covey flushed in browns
tans and whites,
by an almost red fox
sly became a shade intense almost orange.
The scene stirs old scenes
an instantaneous memory of home place
boyhood days.
Thickets of quail bombs exploded,
to fly away free leaving me
awe struck
wondering where they went.
Sometimes a bee or whale or lady bug
came to Harper's mind,
but more often feathers led.
Palette seemed never to go too far
from ROY G BIV,
but every shade of heart hue drawn in

inspires.
Thank you, Charley
for painting what you felt.

In the case of birds, we cannot prove interdependence in these journeys. We also cannot disprove it. In my imagining, it may be communication in flight among and between species, contact calls, that urges another bird on in ways we likely will never know. In a wearying transgulf or hemispheric odyssey, wings do more than flight a single individual, perhaps they uplift others – those flying along with and those of us on the ground looking and listening upward. For all that ornithology can enable us to understand, there is the wonder of the unknown that drives us to want to know more. The knowledge gained and the unknowable that lies unexplained can both put a person in a place to marvel over those dream weaving flocks dodging falling stars.

Mary Oliver, poet laureate of so many of our wild hearts, asked: "…what is it you plan to do with your one wild and precious life?"

I suggest a mantra in response to dear Mary: "Watch. Revere. Repeat."

My professional practice as a cultural and conservation ornithologist, as well as writer, leads me to tell the stories of how we can do better by birds – and how birds can lead us to better understanding of ourselves. My practice is one of conveying how convergences bring worlds into colliding.

Imagine yourselves as a bird.
Take on feathers and wings.
Give up your coarse croaking.
Let your words become   songs and calls.

Imagine. Imagine yourself poised on the edges of a great migration outward into a world of storms. You face headwinds – perhaps, as I do – of hate and bigotry and bias. Stretched out before you is a yawning gulf of difficulty. The distant shores, where you might land, are further away for you and your flocks than they have ever been. The water is less clean. The air is thick and less breathable. The soil is poisoned. Crops won't grow. The wild things below your flight path find fewer places to dwell. Many slide – by individuals, populations, and species – towards a forever imperiled end.

Yet, here you are. You are feeling the zugunruhe – the migratory restlessness – and you are eager though unknowing what the journey across that Gulf of Challenge will hold. Like some migratory bird – wing flicking, chirping – a need to move rules your very life right now and you cannot resist the urge to take off, to leave the certainty and safety of what has been. You must fly off into what might be, could be.

The tailwind of a better future blows warmly at your back. Can you feel it gently ruffling the feathers on your neck? A gust of sudden possibility comes and lifts you from the ground. You flap your wings once, twice, now thousands of times. You look beyond yourself and see before you a dark night, but there are others flown ahead to guide you. Those that have flocked before – author, abolitionist, activist, poet, professor, preacher, teacher. They have identities: Thoreau, Whitman, Douglass, Tubman, Leopold, Carson, Carver, Wilson, Chavez, Seattle, Carter. They have winged on ahead of us in the ink-black sky to show us the way.

We will fly on. It is tiring. Yes, exhaustion buffets and it seems there is no place to land below, only open sea. Wing on. Even as the ground nears and the waves of despair lap at our bellies, threatening to pull us down into the abyss, fly on. Look to your right shoulder and to your left. Know that behind you and before you are others flocking. There are millions flocking in common destination cause – to do better, be better. Now, and going forward. Fly on. Fly on.

Fly on through the long dark night. Perch at dawn. Rest. Sing as the sun rises. Forage. Do it all over again.

Trust that there will be witnesses to your going and becoming.

NOCTURNE

Overhead

   I head the night songs
of thrushes
     the trills
the thrips and wurps
of brown backed birds
     with hopes hitched to stars,
flying on faith of light in the dark.
                        Unseen –
but for the sound of them above
     cleaving ink black sky,

millions of souls riding the wind
to some other world.

I thought them at first dreams
     But for the words the left
in echoes of their wings.

TO KNOW

On the Legacy of Songbird Immigrants, Fifteen and More Million Years Later
David George Haskell

Fugitive sound: your voice it flees
as soon as it arrives.
Tremors in air swallowed by trees
a sonic weave of lives.

Yet fleeting sound is older than stone
deep time lives on in you.
Ancestors' songs in genes are sewn
legends that you renew.

What impulse drove the ancients on
as they left their Asian home –
an urge to gift the dawn with song,
a lust to wing and roam?

Restlessness is generative:
Time infolds, songs relive.

To the Wary Fox Sparrow Rustling in the Leaf Litter

Howie Faerstein

I have never given up on you,
Your sporadic visitations.

Live on through the present extinction.
Never abandon me no matter my home.

Visit me in the third month
Of the year of my death.

Visit me again
In the eleventh month.

Always signal the end of winter
As you mark the beginning.

Oriole
Pepper Trail

Our tropic bird, glowing orange gold,
in black mask, black cape, black beard,
you flaunt your gaudy disguise,
work your way among the willows,
probing the wooly catkins, your beak
quick and keen, flicking aside the fluff,
crushing the sticky buds, drinking
the hidden sweetness there.

For these barely awakened woods,
you left Mexico, those bright blue skies,
soft strange fruits, flew by the stars
to these battered cottonwoods, awkward
limbs drooping high above the water, here
to hang your swaying rebozo, embroidered
nest, safety for the quiet eggs and then the
noisy, sharp-elbowed young.

But it is April still; not yet time to build,
and so you sample spring's meager early feast,
rattle out the songs of first arrival, chase
your rivals twisting through the trees, and
slip through the brambles to the edge
of the stream, where you cool your
burning feathers in these northern waters,
the melted snows of Oregon.

Unbearable Lightness
BJ Buckley

A sparrow weighs
almost nothing.
Before dawn
single digit chill
from spruce shelter
a few are singing

tiny chit-chatter, melody
mumble, almost inaudible –
keening wind,
bone clatter bare branches –
and then as first color
seeps between firmaments

they are feathery smoke
that rises, circles,
sinks down
to the borrow ditch
birds curling their miniature
scaly dinosaur feet

around brittle stems
of winter sere grass,
puffed up like the foam-float
seeds of milkweed, all shades
of the browns and grays
and duns of the earth,

and burdened
by calls unsung and all
of our longing they wait
for the sun and beneath them
the grasses
stand slender and do not bend.

Robins, Runes, Osprey
Gwendolyn Morgan

Take the breath of the new dawn and make it part of you.
It will give you strength.
— JOE COYHIS

We walk along in the dark listening to the robins singing up the
sun into the sky. Snow, hail, rain, sun, the weather a blend of
winter, early spring. The moon intensifies gravitational pulls on
tectonic plates, tidal flows, and our psyches as well. The robins have
a unique happiness song, a repetition of *cheerio* that they sing at
dawn during this time of year. Gradually the other birds join in, a
comforting chorus. The osprey finally returned to Salmon Creek
this week, six osprey at once circling us over the creek, chirping,
whistling, calling, diving for fish. We watch them plunge into water
with their feet first using a reversible front talon and food pads
with tiny spicules for grasping slippery trout and salmon. They
impale the fish upon a broken off branch and fillet it slowly, seem-
ing to enjoy the process of eating too. Occasionally they return
as early as February, and this spring we asked: how do they know
that this year is particularly cold and wet, and to wait until April
to return from Mazatlán, Puerto Vallarta, even Tegucigalpa and
San Salvador? *Raidho* follows the path of the sun, the wheel of
the seasons, the round of life and is a rune of journey, communi-
cation, reunion. Today our neighbor tells us she is nauseous, and
politely declines our offer of clam chowder. The chemotherapy is
cumulative, she reminds us, and this round appears to be taking a
toll. She says clinical journeys are private, painful, often lived alone
without enough support in our isolated culture. She has a circle
of friends and former colleagues who bring soup, crackers, visits,
bird song applications on their *iPods*, a medley of needed things.

Too many others receive unsolicited advice, the recommendations and judgments of those who are scared of the "C" word, worried for their loved ones. She reminds us that we, like the robins, are harbingers of hope too.

The Hummingbird at My Door
Pepper Trail

Spring evening, and here you are, the traveler from Mexico, cold and hungry but not ragged, splendid in fact. Golden-orange raiment, crimson at the throat and so I feed you, of course I feed you. We speak no words, as our languages are not the same, but I give you sweet water, and you eat.

In return you give me the gift of your journey, the vision of those miles, those days on the wing. Last fall, south, every night a new town or patch of wild mountain – peaceful dark or bright and loud beside some highway, big trucks shuddering into the lot, stirring the oleander where you sheltered, enduring the hours til dawn.

Then the desert, and somewhere your invisible wings carried you across the border that seems so real in our imagining. You arrived in the warm winter of that mountain town, Sierra Madre Occidental, all the bright flowers and the day you thought to feed on the red blossom in the girl's hair, and how she ran from you laughing into the arms of a boy.

Then north again, the tilting earth spilling you back into the sky, and you rode that wave of lengthening light that drops you here today, just another town, another yard, but this one with the hanging bottle that, in your language and in mine, means welcome, means traveler's rest, food and drink and shelter for the night.

In the Woods
Jamie K. Reaser

I take long walks in the woods, usually up and down mountain slopes. Usually, alone. Alone in that I'm not in the company of another human. I'm never alone, really. I've known this since I was a little girl in braids. The forest is such good company. It can hold you in ways that people can't, even those who would want to. You can be invisible there, yes, but you can also be seen. I think this is important, this being witnessed. I think we have forgotten about it, witnessing. It is a testament and a salve. It used to be initiation. All the while the birds are singing, we miss it. On the branches of the trees:

"I see you. See me."

Instruction.

Prairie Dreams
J. Drew Lanham

and the clouds sailed above
and the tall grass waved as if ocean
and the blue grosbeaks warbled
and the indigo buntings were not blue
and the goldfinches were more precious than gold
and the grasshopper sparrow had its eye on God
and the meadowlarks were proudly blackbirds
and the bobolinks harmonized in discordance
and the kestrel wind hovered without tiring
and the dickcissels did not disappear
and one bobwhite quail whistled its name
and the kingbird ruled, but did not reign
and none spoke prayers, but sang instead
and all with feathers were angels
 in my prairie dreams.

Commencement
Curt Meine

Where ice meets meltwater, spring commences.
Slightest green tinges the brown grass land.
First crane call echoes off winter's silence.
Meadowlark wings north into a headwind.
Water drips off rooftop, steady to the ground.
The meltwater rising now to the moment.
A stirring deep in the bud, invisible but rousing.
A turning of Earth, slow, inevitable, toward light.
A student, anxious, breaking toward determination.
A world's turmoil bending from blood to purpose.

HERMIT SONG

Kevin Van Tighem

Perhaps it's just natural that a lifelong loner should have an affinity to hermit thrushes. We share a common habitat, after all – that of solitude. But that's too facile an explanation; my love for these birds is more nuanced than that. Whatever the case, when I arrived in the timberline forest near the head of a subalpine basin the other day and stopped to listen again to the wistful beauty of a hermit thrush singing somewhere back in the dim, it evoked a host of memories and associations.

For those who aren't loners, it might seem that loneliness is a stranger to those of us who prefer our own company. Not necessarily. In the late 1970s I landed what seemed the perfect job for one who likes himself better when hanging out with wild things in wild places than with others of his own species. That work – conducting inventories of wildlife populations – took me into the remote corners of Canada's Jasper National Park where I worked by myself, often for days on end. More often than not, when I climbed out of my tent or stepped out of a patrol cabin into the pre-dawn shadows to begin another day of field work, there would be a hermit thrush singing somewhere in the cool secret places beneath the trees. And late in the evening, as mystery spilled down from the peaks to darken the world, again there would be a hermit thrush, intoning its wistful benedictions into a stillness we shared.

The slow, ethereal flutings back in the woods seemed to speak of their own kind of loneliness, of nostalgic loss and poignant rememberings. I'm sure those birds sang for themselves but it was a language I felt I almost understood as I simultaneously savoured my solitude and ached with loneliness. Strange days.

Years earlier, when I was religiously memorizing the first bird book I ever bought – the first edition of *Birds of Alberta*, by Salt and Wilk – I had been taken by the authors' description of the hermit thrush's song: "Oh, heavenly heavenly... ah, holy holy..." I had yet to see my first thrush, but I was haunted never-the-less. Maybe it was those lyrics that first made me equate a shy, brown bird with the parable of human exile from Eden.

Years later, when I was discovering the timberline trails of the Canadian Rockies, I sometimes backpacked with a book to read while resting. Tolkien's *Lord of the Rings* trilogy was a particularly favoured companion; when the larches turned gold or the meadows were brilliant with blooming glacier lilies it was easy to imagine that I was in Middle Earth. In fact, I was – because the tragedy of Middle Earth was the loss of magic from the world of men – but I was discovering places where it lingers on. Jackson Browne sang of an earth wounded by "men who tried to forge her beauty into power" and that, to me, was the metaphor that linked the Christian story of the Fall to Tolkien's fantasy novel: the deep human flaw that makes us all lonely strangers in a world of relations to whom we no longer relate. Magic dies when one ceases to look at the living world with wonder and love, striving to hear its music and to understand how best to relate to the beings with whom we share our existence, and instead simply focus on their utility and how we might possess and use them.

What good is a hermit thrush? Wrong question.

In the story of the Fall, humans eat fruit from the tree of knowledge reserved only for God. But it's not the knowledge that banishes *Homo sapiens* from Eden; it's our reason for wanting that knowledge and the fact that it turns everything else into a mere object of analysis. We objectify the world to gain power over it and, in so doing, isolate ourselves from wonder, humility, and relationship. We make loners of ourselves, and wind up alone, on the wrong side of the gate that locked behind us when we stepped through it. To understand the parable of the Fall, the first thing is to know that it didn't happen once upon a time; it happens every time we look at the world merely as a bundle of resources, rather than a living source of wonder and inspiration.

In Tolkien's trilogy the elves are the ones who love song and mystery, and live in a world infused by magic. "A Elbereth Gilthoniel!" they sing in celebration of a time when all was magic. But at the end, they sail away into the West, taking their magic with them and leaving the world to men. It's the same story, really.

The magic never left; we simply turned away from it. It lives on in an Eden from which we never departed, except in our spirits. It lives in newborn creeks that bubble out of flower-strewn meadows and tumble through forests of larch and fir; it lives among the peaks, especially when they are wrapped in storm clouds or caught in the last rays of the sun; it is in the woods, the fens, the wind, and the wild things. There's a dark magic in the eyes of a grizzly bear when it stands to study a startled hiker, and a bright magic in the way warblers flicker through the willows. Mayflies dance in magic sunbeams. When life emerges out of winter's icy stillness, that's magic. When trees crack with the cold and ravens hunch themselves against the hard winter wind, that's magic too. It's everywhere; it's just hard to see it through the eyes of exiles.

I wonder if hermit thrushes remember the elves, or know them still. I suspect that they are actually birds of Eden, and that the half-light in which they prefer to sing is that place that lies between the lonely, lost world of humankind and the magic from which we turned away. Perhaps, if Tolkien's elves sailed away into the West and left only the memory of magic behind, they also left a humble brown bird to keep that memory alive in sweet, forlorn laments that make mountain shadows sacred.

If we believe that magic has truly left this world, then a hermit thrush's achingly sweet, spiraling song might be heard as the music that arises from memories of memories of mystery. But I think it is more than that; it is proof, in itself that magic never left our world at all; we simply looked away. Back in the sweet, subalpine shadows of forests, those small brown birds lament our loss of wonder even while they invite us back into its embrace.

I've come to the certain belief that there is no time better spent than that spent listening to the hermit thrushes who sing to us from the edge of Eden, reminding us to remember what most of us don't even realize we've forgotten:

"A Elbereth Gilthoniel."

"Heavenly…heavenly…holy…humbly…home."

Black-headed Grosbeak
Walker Abel

Like light through lightless distances
singing comes to everyone.
From beak or mouth, from dark of throat
a melody arises where had been none.

Telescopes can reach the furthest sight
but grosbeak music close to ear
is earth rebounding back to stars
a light evolved into song we hear.

Enchantment of Swifts

Gwendolyn Morgan

Seven Vaux's swifts swirl and dive
gathering insects before they spin into

the neighbor's red brick chimney
slender birds with crescent-shaped wings

round heads, tapered tails
their beaks barely visible even up close

messengers, they invite us to stay as grounded
and elevated as possible in the midst of global chaos

Return to your resonant family, their presence suggests
listen to your feelings, follow your intuition

gray-brown back-lit against the violet-blue sky
rapid aerialists on their way to the Klickitat River

Planes de Renderos, San Salvador
Casa Maria, Carabobo, Venezuela

flying over wildfires, burning sequoias, drought
flood waters rising, the violence of climate change

their bright round eyes intense
they pay attention to every variation of aerial draft

we remember to lift our wings of hope
to watch and listen, advocate and lobby for future generations

trust that whatever is falling away
is opening portals for what is now possible.

Stillness in Perpetual Motion
Faraaz Abdool

This mesmerizing murmuration
With purpose they rise and fall,
Twist and turn.
Together they decide
Whether the time has come to swirl
Into the heavens
Into the void of the night sky
Into an altered state of being –
Metabolism modulated to fit a new frequency
Feet and earth, separated.
Night after night; nutrients shapeshifting
Through muscles and feathers.
Wind feeds blood and wing.

Even if journeying solo;
A bird is never truly alone
For it is tethered to the heavens,
At all times
The fabric of the cosmos
Forms the map by which
That bird is never lost.

And long before
Earth's beloved children return;
Ice is called back
Larvae begin to stir:
The land bears fruit!
Only for tiny, intrepid bodies
To refuel,
To reestablish bonds
With terra firma

And all her affiliates –
Some are food,
Others are homes.

How can the hummingbird exist
Without the flower
And how can the flower exist
Without the hummingbird?
Shared visceral connections,
Inextricably linked,
Impossible to separate.
What was two
Is surely One.

This movement of life
Is the embodiment of
Stillness in perpetual motion.
A contradictory concept
But
Cycles are circular.
There is no beginning
Nor is there an end.
The hands of time are always moving
Yet never leave the confines of the clock.
At every moment there is motion
Yet in totality balance never wavers.

Migratory flyways
Are the bronchi
Of Earth;
Dictated by a gentle planetary waltz
The ebb and flow of life itself,
Migration is the earth breathing.

SURVIVAL LESSONS, POND A16

Richard J. Nevle

From space the curled shape of the San Francisco Bay appears almost embryonic, like some green, liquid thing still becoming itself. At dusk, from the grassy hills east of where I live, the bay looks like someone corralled a swatch of tangerine sky and strung the fenceposts with Christmas lights. Among all the things the bay is, or might be, mostly what I care about on this blue Sunday morning is that it is home to more than a million feathered beings, some 250 species of them. So many have managed to survive, some even thrive among the mosaic of habitats surrounding this wild inlet of the Pacific Ocean, despite the countless ways we've transformed it. This morning, as is so often the case when I seek the company of birds, I'm hoping that I might lose myself in their lives even for just a little while.

It's the heart of midsummer, and I need to get out early if I'm to meet the sunrise. I roll my bike out the back door and turn onto hushed streets. Even though I live in the middle of a big, sprawling city, the sky is still dark enough to make out the tiny disks of Saturn, Jupiter, and Mars arranged in the neat arc of the ecliptic. Bright stars of constellated birds, the Eagle and the Swan, shimmer overhead.

My headlamp pierces the cool morning, the beam strobing off street signs. I pedal down a thoroughfare which in a few hours will be thick with traffic. But now it's early enough that there are only a few cars about, workers returning home or heading to jobs at medical clinics, restaurant kitchens, nursing homes. Caretakers of the world, their dimly lit faces glowing behind window glass. I pass the county jail and cross a low bridge, then turn onto a path that drops into an arroyo thick with sycamores and willows. I pedal northwest, following the dark current of the Guadalupe River, named in honor of a woman who appeared on a small hill near Mexico City in 1531, her body radiating, according to legend, a shimmering corona of light. The air turns cooler in the arroyo cradling the river, carrying the scent of wood smoke. A small fire flickers out in front of a plywood shack, one of several in an encampment built by those who simply can't afford the rent elsewhere.

As I near the bay, the wind carries the licorice scent of fennel and the funk of mud and brine. I turn north toward a mosaic of salt evaporation ponds in the Don Edwards San Francisco Bay National Wildlife Refuge. About ninety percent of the native tidal marshes of the San Francisco Bay, the largest estuary on the west coast of the Americas, have been diked and drained for conversion into farmland and pasture – and in the southern reaches of the bay – into salt evaporation ponds. A massive, ongoing restoration campaign aims to convert most of the salt ponds back to native marshland. But restoration is never straightforward. For one thing, in the decades since the ponds were cordoned off from the bay by levees, some birds have adapted. A variety of avian species took up nesting in the evaporation ponds, including Forster's terns, whose fuzzy, semi-precocial young I hope to spy this morning.

One of the ponds, Pond A16, envelops an archipelago of artificial islands. It was hoped that the islands, which were carefully designed to include a number of features previously shown to foster nesting success, would help compensate for the loss of prime habitat resulting from pond conversion elsewhere. Before the islands were built, A16 supported a colony of several hundred nesting terns. But after the pond was drained, the islands dredged up from bay-bottom muck, and the bay subsequently allowed to flush back in, the terns didn't return. Instead they took up attempting to raise families in an adjacent marsh, where land-based predators had easy access. Only a fraction of the nestlings survived. At least until scientists began deploying so-called social attraction measures on the islands, which included the strategic deployment of fifty decoys – painted by local schoolchildren to mimic Forster's terns – and an array of speakers that broadcasted audio recordings of a clamorous tern colony. The intervention worked, and the number of terns nesting in Pond A16 is on the rise. The survival rate of the pond's hatchlings is now twice that of the adjacent marshland.

When Forster's terns arrive in the bay in April from their wintering grounds in Southern California and Mexico – some traveling from as far as Guatemala – the shell and raincloud-colored migrants are dressed in their dashing breeding plumage. They've cast off the rakish aviator's goggles worn in winter, and instead don jet-black pirates' masks. Their dark bills have turned to the incandescent orange of molten iron, save for their ink-dipped tips. They're habanero-hued legs are just as outlandish.

Forster's terns are devil-may-care birds. They are little flying zorros, they are swashbucklers on the wing. They plunge headfirst into the water to snatch small silver fish, which they grasp with dagger-tipped beaks. With sleek, sharp wings they bank in dizzying hairpin turns. On the wing a tern will sometimes voluntarily drop its prey, only to dive down and pluck it back from the air, as if just for the hell of it, as if just because it can. When on the hunt, and another of its kind ventures near, it will scold and harangue the rival with skittering bleats and clicks and give chase. Get too close to a nest, and the bird will dive-bomb you. Once I saw an Arctic tern draw blood from the scalp of a friend who inadvertently approached too near, transgressing some invisible boundary. Though

I've yet to see Forster's terns resort to such extremes, I'm not about to test the ferocity of their protective instincts.

As I approach the ponds, I discover that the levee trail that affords access to Pond A16 is closed off for construction. Trucks and heavy equipment are strewn across the levee, the machines docile in the early morning, tiny as toys amidst the bay's shimmering vastness. I'll have to navigate a maze of causeways if I'm to have a hope of getting within viewing distance of the tern babies.

I watch the terns hunt as I ride. The birds cast their gazes downward as their wings row the air with deep, powerful strokes. A line from The Windhover – a poem by the 19th century Jesuit poet Gerard Manley Hopkins – comes to me. Watching a kestrel in flight, Hopkins writes of his "heart in hiding / Stirred for a bird, – the achieve of, the mastery of the thing!" One of the terns I'm watching hovers over the water, its tail spread wide in a scissoring fan backlit by the sky, its under plumage brilliant white against the blue. The tern looks like some tiny, powerful, radiant being. The tern looks like some small, fierce angel of death.

In the last lines of The Windhover, Hopkins describes "blue-bleak embers" as they fall from a fire and "gall themselves, and gash gold-vermillion." Death, for this poet-priest, offered the possibility of a luminous reincarnation. This has always been true. For once our time has run its course, our remains – if we are lucky enough – might be laid down near a tree. Its roots might find us. Our bones might become branches. Our eyelashes might become the veins of leaves. We might become the bodies of earthworms; we might be given wings.

The other day, biking to work along the bay, I saw a Forster's tern zip past not two feet in front of me, the curve of a fish, limp and shimmering, in its bill. The bird winged toward what I thought might be a nest of hungry fledglings. This, I know, is the way of things. The body of a fish might become a fuzzy baby tern. The baby tern might nurture a California gull or a red fox or maybe a marauding rat. But there's a good chance too that the nestling will survive to adulthood.

In the word survival, the prefix sur means over or above, as in crossing a bridge over and above some danger or hardship. As a young child, the poet Javier Zamora survived a nine-week odyssey of migration, much of it alone, traveling from his native El Salvador through Guatemala and Mexico and then walking across the scorching Sonoran desert into Arizona. He writes of surviving by throwing rocks at the fruits of saguaro cacti and eating their fallen, red, syrupy flesh. To survive, Zamora has written, is to over-live.

I try to imagine what the bay once was, centuries before everything changed. Jade sloughs meandering endless expanses of marshland beneath a fog-lidded sky. White mounds of shells rising near Ohlone villages. Smoke drifting from campfires. The wind carrying the laughter of children. Grizzly bears lumbering across the wetlands, drawn to the oceanic scent of a whale carcass washed ashore. Flocks of birds wheeling overhead like feathered clouds, their throngs so numerous you might pluck one from the sky.

This morning, as I bike across the bay's transformed wildness, white pelicans gulp fish from salt pond water and swallow them whole. The birds know what they must do to survive. As for myself, there are too many days I spend spinning in worry, anxious about work, lamenting the world we're losing, lamenting what I'm losing as I age – rather than being grateful for what still remains. I think I might be under-living too much of the time.

I never quite make it to Pond A16. My workaround route fails; the trail juncture is gated off, the pond inaccessible. The tern colony is visible through my binoculars, but the distance is too great to make out any chicks. They're too well camouflaged. Good for them. May they survive. May their wings grow sleek and strong and carry them safely to southern wintering grounds. May they return, again and again.

This is what I want to remember: that any of us get a chance at all. That survival is its own kind of miracle. I want to over-live with whatever breath of time might be left. And when death comes, let it be as a sharp-billed tern, snatching life like quicksilver from the brine.

Swallow Flight
Steve A. Patterson, Jr.

There the streaming swallows go,
barn and *bank* only, tonight,
twisting above field
in the twi-lit coolness
of pre-autumn's wind,
flying into darkness,
slipping in the night past
destinations unchosen,
aiming vaguely, easily,
toward a place
that smells like south.

It's a traffic of feathers
whipping gentle eddies
of unbreathed air,
birds occupying night trails
'til morning gravity
strengthens its pull
toward sky's terrestrial partner.

Home is not a place
but a time of day,
a fatigue in the wings,
a decision made by
swallows in the flight.
Home is the distance between
memory and premonition.
There swallows incubate powerlines
until breezy begging prevails
and they tango
once again with the sky.

The Fisherbird
Bill Hilton Jr.

Shady, placid pond edge, mud bank exposed by drought. A heron, sleek and gray, lifts its foot and freezes, claws just touching water, yellow eyes wide, neck pulled back tightly, serpentine. This spring-loaded trap, primed with dagger bill, awaits the swim-by of hapless bass or brim. The heron lowers raised foot slowly, plants it on pond bottom, stabilizing what comes next. Soon prey glides near and stops, alert, but not enough. Patient marksman, motionless, the heron waits, then strikes with lightning speed and brutal force, both deadly aimed as one more fish goes down the craw of our stealthy, long-legged wader.

Loon
Sidney Wade

Designed
in cold

beautiful lines.
Brilliantined

black head,
fire-red eyes

that defy
the darkness

of the water
in which it thrives.

In pure lines
it dives

for lively
prey, lightning

in black,
as it sweeps

its waterways
with sharp eyes.

At home in deep
cold water,

at home in the dome
of the sky,

at home in flight
as it roams

from summer
to winter,

its unearthly cries
haunt our sleep.

They bring splinters
of wildness

to our nights
as we navigate

through dreams
and the streaming

wakes of the trails
we earthlings make.

Living on James Wright
Derek Sheffield

As they aim their laser pens
over charts, ornithologists calmly explain
the slow, sloping descent
of neotropical migrants.
They open factual arms in dim rooms
to show the size of Ohio – puckering widows
and one dirty river become the yardstick
for South America's clear-cuts.

If he were here, he would catch
the yellow warbler
that clutched my hand today, its
song of hurried sweets.
As he broke his lines for the warm
tap of its heart, a hobo
would appear, and a boy with rusty hair,
a real deadeye, sighting
down a secret barrel for one more
slurred silhouette.

Even the blips of northbound vireos
along the branch between Americas
would cast in his lyric a green wing.
I heard him once, a lone Ohioan
opening his throat

three thousand miles from the gathering
outlines of his state. And when
that yellow warbler lay
in my palm, thinned from its journey,
a breath of fierce light searching me

with one dark eye, I stood
as if I did not breathe
and only wind could move me.

Nighthawks
Jan Lamberg

A Course in Miracles defines
a miracle as a lapse in time and space.
Miracles, I don't know
but the coursing through lapses in time and space,
yes – beginning mid-August,
when I look up after dinner,
just before dusk, dew sifting
 flying ants, nighthawks
 glide twist flutter-flip.
Some force other than
wind breath our planet's orbit
tips our northern continent into autumn,
buffets nighthawks aloft.
 Sky, their earth,
 clouds, their fields,
canopies of my catalpa-lined street
& white-pined river banks
all point to their thick white bands.
Near-night's bevy of haze-combers
I stand taller for you too;
never one to clap,
too eager to bow,
a lightning rod grounded –
 can you feel me awestruck...?
Your white-plumed undercarriage needs no heft
you herd snacks whiskers-to-gullet
from my poison-free garden groomers...
 maybe
you hear my head snap off its neck,
my voice incapable of wow,
I breathe finally into your wing-work –
 Aaahhhh....

Thrush Love
J. Drew Lanham

In an attempt
to make my worn suburban
surroundings more thrush-philic
I've let things go past "maintenance".
Let things grow beyond containers
or neat bed borders.
Opened the door
to what some would call "weeds".
Welcomed all feathered things olive-backed
and skulky.
Rolled out a welcome mat of disarray.
Made glimpses of pieces
and parts of what might be,
the priority.
I've let the dank rank higher than bright.
Encouraged shadows to persist
at all hours.
Let snails have right of way.
Asked the olive-backed birds
if warblers and other night travelers might find
such an ill-kempt place to their liking.
Ferns, four-o'clocks, sumac, poke salad
and yes even un-American things like privet
find function here,
so long as the trans-gulf travelers approve.
Gray cheeked-esque, Swainsonii-like
or wood-ishness not withstanding,
Could a Bicknell find my spot inviting?
But then I would only know
if it chose to speak.
My goal in enhancing thrushiness

has not been to increase any lists,
but more simple want, desire
wish.
To be a spot on the map below
starlit transit,
that by dawn is worthy of
a pause to snatch a nap's wink
or late worm.
A link in some chain of a chance to make it
further South
to perhaps return again.

El Palpitar del Planeta (The Planet's Pulse)
Carlos Galindo-Leal

Cuando concluye el verano
y el otoño lo releva,
es tiempo de que me atreva
a emprender vuelo lejano

When summer ends
and autumn relieves him
it's time for me to dare
to undertake a distant flight

Más vale iniciar temprano,
antes que el frio aparezca
y la luz del sol fallezca
reduciendo el alimento

Better start early
before the cold appears
and the sunlight fades
reducing the feed

¡Volaré hacia el firmamento!
sin que nada me entorpezca

I will fly into the firmament!
without any hindrance

En esta anual travesía
chorlos, playeros, charranes,
halcones y gavilanes
migramos en sintonía

On this annual journey

plovers, sandpipers, terns,
falcons and hawks
we migrate in unison

Y volando en jerarquía
patos, gansos y cercetas,
pelícanos en saetas,
chipes y calandrias bellas

And flying in hierarchy
ducks, geese and teals,
pelicans in arrows,
warblers and beautiful orioles

Vuelan bajo las estrellas
disfrutando los cometas

They take wing under the stars
enjoying the comets

Después de una larga estancia
en un entorno contrario,
del lugar originario
regresa la itinerancia

After a long stay
in an environment opposite
to the place of origin
the roamers return

No es una extravagancia,
la primavera indiscreta
con luz y calor inquieta
el instinto milenario

It's not an extravagance,
spring indiscreet
with light and heat
the ancient instinct arouses

que lleva el ritmo primario
del palpitar del planeta

that carries the primal rhythm
of the planet's pulse

The River in Autumn
Jamie K. Reaser

You have to know the river to know how she feels when her banks
are emptying of song. You have to have gone to her through the
seasons and listened to the waters talking – rocks as tongues over
and around which they lap. I listened to the river this morning,
not long after the old Harvest Moon had set herself to waning,
when the low storm clouds – thick, grays, and meaningful – held
back just enough rain for just long enough to go to her damp
woodland buffer in search of ripe pawpaws and spicebush berries
and the small birds, feathers blanding, intent on departure because
something beyond the telling of science or poetry possesses them
to reorient everything about their lives: true South. Common yel-
lowthroat. Blue-gray gnatcatcher. That summer tanager I adored
all summer. Chip notes and screes now in the golden wingstem
and grape vines and box elder. Shortly, the river will run her course.
These birds go well beyond her reach. She has to wait.

Before the dams, spring returned both the birds and the rockfish.

Autumnal
Shaun T. Griffin

In this time the sun skirts
low in the south and the rabbitbrush
bathes in amber light,
the mountain crumbles to color
and the cinnamon-sky
stirs the leaves to ground.

The quiet, above all else,
lifts bird song to the ear –
a house sparrow etches the wild rose,
a downy woodpecker thrums the pine bark
into a thousand particles of sound
and the whippoorwill swallows an early dusk.

What I have to lay down before them –
these small tools of science
will not identify such joy. Oh certain virtue,
the day is not over and what sound
there is predates all mind
and will remain its eternal companion.

Even after they are gone.

Autumn River Music
Hap Wilson

From the red and gold amongst bedrock folds
When the ferns and rushes brown,
And the north wind sings on frigid wings,
As leaves come tumbling down.
The loons still call from spring to fall
With ancient voices reverberate,
From lake to pond and hills beyond
To pause and boldly hesitate.

The cold north chill that tempers the will
And the time to leave draws near,
Each seasoned bird recalls the word
That comes each time of year.
To migrate south to Mississippi's mouth
And find pleasure in the sun,
Where warming rays and moonbeams play
Until winter time is done.

Then there are those like ravens and crows
And jays both blue and grey,
Who spend their time in wintery pine
Content enough to stay.
The snowy owl and partridge fowl
Both while away the hours,
Predator and prey they all know their way
When winter storms devour.

From Hudson Bay and glades far away
The geese and cranes take flight,
Too harsh the north when fall draws forth
To stay would seal their plight.

When leaves change colour they tell each other
That now's not the time to take lightly,
Although it is hard to leave their backyard
The temperature will always drop nightly.

But what might we feel if something would steal
Those birds that sing of love,
Could be man's greed cause the lack of good feed
To blacken the skies up above.
Climate change they say will darken the day
And our birds will fly no more,
The future reveals how we act to conceal
What needs to be done before.

What the Bird Knows
Frank Inzan Owen

The hermit doesn't sleep at night,
in love with the blue of the vacant moon.
The cool of the breeze that rustles the trees rustles him too.
— CHING AN (1851-1912)

What can busy red dust men say about a bird? Do any of them consider birds at all? The red dust men are always rushing around counting and stacking their coins. They don't know about colors and wing-shapes, songs and calls, migration routes or the placement of aeries and roosts on high. I can hear the busy red dust men barking on and on about the Dow rather than the Dao, with no thought of the millions of birds migrating through the skies over their sleep-filled September night. Red dust men aren't like us who glow, quiet, in the silent blue night of pine winds. We sit up half the night with old poems and rice wine, faithfully keeping the moon company, waving farewell as warblers and thrushes begin their departure. Busy red dust men are loaded down with worries and frenzy, projections and details.

Details aren't bad. Details can be good. They help us learn. Learn about life. Learn about death. When to plant tomatoes. Details are among the teachings of the Bird Tribes. They invite us to pay soft-attention. Learn a few songs. That's a gray catbird! That's a cerulean warbler! Learn the color of crowns. That's a ruby-throated hummingbird! That's a dark-eyed junco! Learn a few markings on wings. That's a nighthawk!

But some kinds of details are always from the outside. The outside. The outside looking from the outside. To really know a bird you can't be one of those busy red dust men, rushing and scurrying, eating up the world like a deranged termite. To really know a bird, you have to slow down. You have to slow down to Bird Time. You have to slow down to the rhythm of the feathered ones. To really know a bird you have to become one; and to become one you have to embrace the bird-part of your own dreamingbody – the part that sees and sings and knows how to fly, the part that knows the holiness of idleness, the part that is intimate with clouds and up-drafts, the part that is aware-but-fearless, the part that knows of spiraling and tumbling, the part in-tune – always-in-tune – with the vast bounty gained by sitting silently in the rain.

Talk to a poet about all this. They'll tell you, I'm sure, that to know a bird you have to become a bird, and to become a bird you have to enter the bird. You have to enter the bird to know what the bird knows. You have to shift your shape to understand ancient bird philosophy. To know a bird, to really know a bird, you have to embrace what the bird knows. When you do, then you are free.

The Small Birds: An Almanac
John Lane

I

This morning I watch the small birds swerve and flutter through the trees above me along the road. I know these trees are called swamp maples, though the swamp is down the hill.

Some say *Acer rubrum* to show off.

Today these trees form an early smorgasbord, a climate crisis casserole, these first first blooms, these buds, these developing samaras, and the small birds have moved in. The branches form a hazy mist to munch above, and the mixed flock feasts.

So these trees have a name and I know it. But the small birds conceal who they are. Distance is their trench coat today.

2

Hilton Head Island

In the sea islands the large wading birds are easy to spot— feeding in the sloughs, cruising over roadways. But in the piedmont the small birds stay hidden among the fans of palms. To track the small birds you have to slow down, to attend to every moment, to listen.

This morning the small birds are winged olive bodies no bigger than walnuts. Sometimes they are shadows amplifying avian mystery.

To stay silent on the names of the small birds is to confirm them. Names came late, maybe as little as 200,000 years ago, maybe later. Before there were names for the small birds there was their personality, habitat, range, and diets. There was seasonal plumage.

3
Back Home

By not naming the birds I see them clearer. I stain the signal of their presence a shocking hue through silence.

The small tufted birds, the black-capped birds, the gray, wing-bar birds, the muffin brown birds with twitching tails. The small birds that browse the ground, and the ones that hide in branches above the water dish. The seed-stirred birds who wait until I fill the tube. These are some of the birds moving through my yard.

Migration
Rob Jackson

Where mountains and valleys undulate
and the Great Basin drains to one salt lake,
where shadscale and sagebrush shelter prey,
you settled in a juniper, bark peeling
like flesh stripped from the ground
squirrel in your talons.
Months wandered through days of plenty,
each updraft a banking of wings.
When nights lengthened
and Aquila ended its summer passage,
you departed. I prepared for your flight,
turning south in expectation.

You passed overhead as I stood in light
rain of the isthmus, waiting for quetzals that never came.
I swore off bird quests, gave my book to a boy
who craved photos and English-Spanish names
to make him a naturalist.
He offered his skiff in return, one chance to catch a boat-
billed heron's *kwok* through mangroves,
skim past basking crocodiles
so close the slits of their pupils
stood tall as trees opening into darkness.
For a time, I refused to look skyward.

Storms blew your forebears
to the Galápagos. Their lores
turned blue-gray like the prickly-pear trees
they perched on, ceres and talons
petal-yellow in the equatorial sun.
I followed with the winds.

In austral spring you landed in a sea
of grass, waves coursing plains.
You lingered, watched tufts of guanaco hair
flick like tail feathers on ombu bark
as the Pampero's first breath blew northwards.
Three months you waited
at peace with rheas on the ground.

In February you faced north,
retracing your path
over the Andes' golden rivers
to pass through the Valley of the Oaxaca
and regain the steppe, sagebrush leaves
brimmed with melting snow.
I followed in restlessness,
restlessness blanketing the earth.

TO WONDER

The Western Tanager or Why Montana
Sean Hill

Piranga ludoviciana

Are wanderings the same as migrations?
I came to Montana for love, which sometimes is
how we know our destinations.

The western tanager flies here for procreation
when the snow goes wet, puddles, runs, and takes to
far wandering. Is this the same as migration?

A life is the sum of grand and modest peregrinations.
Communities bloom at the meeting of opportunity
and ambition and can be a way to know our destinations.

A fire-engine red head cooling to orange to
a sunny yellow body with those charcoal wings,
the male western tanager flashes conflagration

or an eastern autumn, in flight. One, familiar, greeted
me shortly after we both arrived letting me know
our wanderings weren't the same – his, a migration.

In a stand of ponderosas where a snow blanket lay for decades
or longer, the dendrologist says the trees moved up from what's
Mexico as that quiet water pulled back, a different migration

– moving seed by seed north generationally migrating
to where they had been and where they could live
never asking *how do we know our destination?*

Why Montana? One among my interrogations,
both public and private like *How big is a home?*
Are wanderings the same as migrations?
and *How do I know my destinations?*

Do Branches Delight?
Jamie K. Reaser

Do branches delight in the bird? Do they hold tight to the nest, feeling proud and responsible? Do they believe the singing is for them – a lyrical prayer for a long life, or maybe a blessing as gratitude – reciprocity? Is it coincidence that their leaves come and go as the birds come and go?

Do birds delight in the watcher? Do they feel seen in the way that humans long to be seen? Do they take note of form and behavior – field characteristics? Do they want our affections, or are mornings for them about the fullest extent of their tolerance – for some short, for others long? Are we to be unrequited lovers? Oh, my dearest, no – I have reason to believe that we keep rising early and showing up in edgy places because we've had the experience of something looking into our eyes and choosing to stay for a while. Choosing our company. Choosing us.

I go to the woodland, the meadow, and the water's edge with hopes and dreams, with just enough knowledge to pry the magic loose from the breaking day. When I lift the binoculars, it can be science and it can be mythos – simultaneously. Don't take one with you unless you bring the other. It's a rose-breasted grosbeak and it's a god whose heart bleeds, his lament for the soul of man too great to be contained within his feathered chest.

In the branches, there is song.

Wilson's Warbler
Derek Sheffield

Twin engines full throttling
a boat crowded with people

glassing rolling ocean
in every direction.

They really want to see
the strange, long-winged birds

they haven't, and check
their long, strange names. But here,

dropping in from the white sky,
a little yellow one

matching their speed
and flapping for all its worth

in the wrong direction,
thirty inexplicable miles out

and counting. Of the few
who raise their binoculars,

the first to see through
the blur of its wings

shouts into the wind two words
they will later read on a list.

Wait for Dawn
Maggie Clifford

I can hear your song
Though you left me here alone
I look for you each morning
But all I see is stone
All I see is stone

Sometimes it seems you were never here
Your voice is but a dream
Barren branches greet me now
Along this mountain stream
Along a mountain stream

What could I do?
But watch you fly away
What could I do?
What could I say?
My words could never keep you
My hands are not a cage
I thought the pain of letting go
Would soften as I age

The longer you are gone from me
The more I need you here
Please tell me as the seasons change
You'll return to me, my dear
Return to me, my dear

One day say you'll return to me
As you've done before
At dawn you will return to me

And sing to me once more
Please sing to me once more

What could I do?
But watch you fly away
What could I do?
What could I say?
My words could never keep you
My hands are not a cage
I thought the pain of letting go
Would soften as I age

Now I walk these lonesome mountains
I wonder where you've gone
Sweet sorrow takes me over
And so I wait for dawn
So I wait for dawn

Merlin Medicine
J. Drew Lanham

In certain light the land writhes. It ripples under the newborn winter wheat where the plow has gone. In that nearing solstice glow, a little merlin perches atop a lichen-splotched post; soaks up what sun lingers. They are I think, the boldest falcons. Size does not matter to a merlin. It believes itself to be at least twice the raptor it is. As I watched this bird, maybe come in on the last cold front, I wonder if it thinks on a twilight killing? A pipit or palm warbler, newly arrived from some near top-of-the-world-wild-place, would be suitable sunset snack.

Easy slow pickin's. I can believe that it has also likely considered the meadowlarks still calling as suitable selections on the all-you-can-catch menu. The merlin's presence explains the fence line's sparrowlessness. I snap photos and my mind whirs with the exposures. The merlin turns. Head bobs, then stares back at the lens, passing quick judgement on the single eye rudely returning the stare. It falls from the tall utility line pole and vectors westward. I can only guess what decision was made in the exchange between camera iris and predatory eyes. I leave the guessing to find the next bird. Twilight is my time more than early morning or midday. Possibilities grow in the lowering night before seeing disappears. Land and birds. Sun and sky. It is daily necessity, as crucial a prescription to be filled as any bottle might hold. Today's dose of merlin has made me feel much, much better about my own identity, or misgivings of such.

Red-headed Woodpecker
Shaun T. Griffin

Sun was low on the eastern sky –
    a crack in the horizon and the occasional
        wing disturbed the quiet. My friend

stood with the camera on the rock outcropping:
    a red-tailed hawk nested overhead.
        I thought it enough to find a raptor

in the binoculars but my friend waved
    down-canyon: in the cottonwoods
        forked off a broken branch

the gift came into view: the scarlet cap,

the white wings, the raucous *kwrrk*
    sailing from its beak. Blown
        two thousand miles off course

this woodpecker migrated from Mexico
    to the West. Not Kansas, not home
        to provide, but Six Mile Canyon –

runneled with gold tailings and a crick
    of treated water, here in the incomplete West –
        regal as sunlight, perched in a web of wood,

this stopping ground, this canyon of greed
    and grief, how is it you opened your arms
        to a chrysalis of color this April day?

It's Complicated
Rob Jackson

There was a time it wasn't,
when days eddied like the Blacksmith Fork
and even love was simple,
when we could fit everything we owned
in the trunk and the back seat
of an airplane was a blessing,
when the term papers were read
and the grades submitted on the lark
sparrows' return each May and the lab,
a yellow, could hunt, when grousing
was up and down the mountain,
punching through avalanche chutes
seeking the whirr of wings and a clear shot
of tequila was enough, with umbrellas
unthinkable, a bow to starched shirts and nine to five
meant a straight or softball or a night of love.
Did we know we were swapping "baby" for baby,
trucks for wagons, and sleeping bags for hotels,
that we'd start telling stories in the past tense,
peddle that Chevy Monza with no heat
but just enough room for an inline 4
and a trunk that beckoned
like an elephant?
We could go home if we chose,
fly with the swallows,
follow the pink elephant
heads that bloom when the snow finally clears
at Tony Grove Lake, their leaves supple as young ferns.
The swans and laughter may return,
this spring, or the fall after.

Query for Owl at Spring Equinox
William Pitt Root

Rainpocks in
old snow
                    black twigs
drenched
                    in lunar sheen

Owl, from what perch tonight,
claw-clenched,
rinsed in drizzle,
will you drift that haggard single vowel
you've stolen from the moon?

☀

Whichever humdrum suburb
you haunt,
                    your autumnal
presence – reminiscent of dry leaves
and warm fur twitching
        in your grasp –
will occupy innumerable dreams
with grim wonder
you know perfectly well
as you cry your muted cry across the sleepers.

☀

Puffed up like some Diogenes
overly aware
        of your familiar errand,
your fingers gone to claws

on this endless quest,
your ancient eyes
        lamps of their own,
you know perfectly well
        we who begin as dreamers
close our lives
in sleep
and yet on those lips of horn
always the same question
asked in the same key.

Yours is the angelic race
from reptiles evolved,
winged raptors conjured
out of subtle cunning
and its curse.
              From which
of the mineral-eyed
have you arisen, your scales
elongated into quills, your head
great as the moon
now warm-blooded in you, ravenous
for an answer to your query,
the insatiable rhetoric
of your unwringable neck?

Only your
dry tongue, exposed
as you hiss
at us, hints
of your origin.

※

I ask you, Owl,
ask you
as new rain falls
on old snowpack
beneath twigs shrunken dark:

How far have you come?

How far do you mean to go?

New Paltz, New York

THE VISITOR

Richard J. Nevle

> *And sore must be the storm*
> *That could abash the little bird*
> *That kept so many warm.*
> – FROM HOPE IS A THING WITH FEATHERS
> BY EMILY DICKINSON

A gauze of clouds hung low in the sky, veiling a crescent moon. The plaintive calls of goldfinches filtered in through an open window, and the air smelled of cold spring rain. My laptop keys fluttered out a gentle rhythm as I readied myself for another day of remote teaching and meetings, the glowing images of my students' faces confined to squares on a computer screen. It was May, still early on in the pandemic, and each morning as I worked from my living room couch, I could hear the world waking outside my window. The goldfinches were predictable among the many neighborhood regulars singing in the half-lit darkness. But spring brings newness and one morning, quite suddenly, there was something unusual, something strange, a sound I'd never heard before. Or if I had, it hadn't registered in my half-conscious brain as anything worth attending to. Even then when I heard it, I'm ashamed to admit,

I tried to ignore the sound, as I needed to focus and prepare for class. But then it happened again, a high, liquidy squeak, like the creaking of a wheel on a wooden toy. And then again: *pik pik pik pik pi-pi-pi pipipipik. Pik pik pik pik pi-pi-pi pipipipik.* The call descended in pitch and then accelerated, like someone was trying to tell me a story but kept getting overly excited at the end. Movement twitched in my peripheral vision. My concentration broke. I looked up from my computer screen and out the window.

I softened my focus. Widened my gaze. Watched for movement. And there it was. A bright lemony crescent of a bird with olive wings, the feathered creature almost hidden where it perched among a chaos of green leaves. The bird flitted from twig to twig, skittering like electricity. Some spark of recognition said *warbler*, and then the vague sense of familiarity sharpened as the bird's flickering movement revealed a black skull cap and a flash of obsidian eyes – Wilson's warbler. The tiny bird had called me to attention. *And just exactly what,* I wondered, *was it doing outside my window?*

My mind flew back to my first warbler encounter only a few years before, in the Sierra Nevada, on a walk with a dear friend, a ranger who migrates each summer to the Yosemite high country. On seeing the creature, she told me the story of the bird's long and arduous journey. And so I knew the warbler who'd landed outside my little house in the Bay Area must have come from very far, journeying from its wintering home in Mexico or Central America, guided by starlight, chutzpah, and wits. It seemed a blessing, this warbler's cheery arrival in the midst of the gray year of lockdown, when I, like so many others, could not safely travel to visit loved ones far away. The tiny bird had stopped to rest, and before evening, I knew, it would be gone, continuing its journey, perhaps to the same patch of subalpine forest where I'd first seen its kind.

Later in the morning, after my wife and daughter woke, I took them outside to show them our sloe-eyed visitor. It turned out there were a pair of them – darting among the branches of our neighbor's fruit trees. As I showed my daughter how to follow their calls and spot them, I mentioned their journeys of thousands of miles. *That's insane, Dad. How can such a tiny bird travel so far? How fast does it fly? How long does it take them?*

Bird migration is an act of defiance. Of resistance. The migrants must overcome such grave dangers – disappearing habitat, declining food supply, collisions with skyscrapers, predation by roaming cats – to mention only a few of the deadly threats they face on their breathtaking odysseys. They fly toward a future in which the odds are slim, a future in which even their most concentrated force of effort cannot guarantee survival. When we give ourselves just one minute to contemplate the sheer audacity of a warbler's astonishing act of migration, how can we not be moved by this bird, this diminutive winged superhero, who weighing no more than an apricot, flies some 2000 miles just to have a chance at a future? How can we not leap to our feet, hearts in our throats, and applause?

A Wilson's warbler might complete its roundtrip journey half a dozen times over the span of its fleeting life. Like so many of its migrating avian relatives, the warbler is drawn annually from the tropics by burgeoning insect populations that emerge in high northern latitudes during the boreal spring and summer. There are other reasons too. "Every living thing has the same wish to flourish again and again," wrote Craig Childs in his book *Animal Dialogues*. "Beyond that, our differences are quibbles." Perhaps the warblers long for peaceful lullabies of mountain streams to soothe their just-hatched young. Perhaps they seek a sense of safety and protection offered by the branches of evergreen forests. When they arrive at last in some high, pine-scented destination, do they feel a sense of belonging, of homecoming?

To be a migratory bird is no easy thing. It is a life full of challenges I cannot begin to fathom. But even so, as I spent day after day gazing at a computer screen in the confining comfort of my living room, I wanted to be like this brave wanderer, to be a feathered thing moving through the wind, propelled by breath and wings and beating heart on a long journey over moonlit mountains and silver rivers, the star-glittering sky guiding my path. I wanted to be a thing with feathers, to sing with full-throated ease, to forget the misery of the pandemic, to shed my fear of the infinitesimal, to escape the anxious worry of what the virus might do to me or those I loved as they labored on the frontlines.

I'd never seen a Wilson's warbler, much less any warbler in the tangled green oasis that is my backyard. Perhaps they'd come in previous years, a few individuals pausing to rest and forage in the scrim of gangly trees outside my window, but I simply hadn't been present to greet them. On any other morning before the pandemic, I would have been up rushing to ready myself for work, then racing off downtown on my bike to catch an early train north to the university campus where I teach. Once on board, I would have caught my breath, gazed out the window, looked east toward the sunrise as the blur of the world hurtled by, thinking of the day ahead, thinking of the long list of tasks that would need my attention. Or perhaps I would have been dreaming, as I so often do, of clambering up some slope of talus, of moving skyward, my body loose and open to the movements of animals and the wind, to the come-hither gazes of alpine wildflowers, to the feathery breath of clouds, to the sound of water trickling over stones.

But on that early morning in May, I'd been stuck at home, in just the right place it turned out. A winged visitor had come from half a world away, perched outside my window, and sang its wild, thrilling song to anyone present to listen. The warbler was, of course, only being itself. But when it opened its sharp, small beak to sing, some deep-down thing stirred, reawakening an ancient yearning for a wider sense of kinship with the world. When I see some green-gold warbler flitting among leaves, how can I not long to join its kind, if not as one of them, if not capable of flight or of its song spun from liquid tropical sunlight, then at least as a devoted ally? When we see a thing with feathers perched on a branch, is it not a beckoning to what could be? An invitation to inhabit a geography of hope, an invitation to live in a world in which we and warblers both might flourish?

Nest from Above//Nest from Below
Erin Robertson

from hummingbird-height

I'd been weaving webs together
respinning silk in small circles
packing cottonwood down
into a soft round cup
for most of the morning before they came:
noisy, boisterous, cracking the calm –
the who-mens – two small ones
wearing caps with their own broad bills

I'd no time to watch their wrestling
zipped in and out
with light loads
darning my knit nest
with a needle of beak
beyond the reach of their
wooden swords and endless tussle

but, it couldn't be helped –
my emerald sheen flashed too bright
through fir branch –
they knew me at once –
their faces grew holes
and sucked air in

from the ground

despite their eager pointing
I couldn't see til liftoff
when her body uncoupled from tree,
became bird
buzzed across blue like broken green glass

my eyes, distracted by her spark,
had to search the limbs again
finally found the slumped-open bowl
she'd been busily turning
on a flimsy branch right over sidewalk
likely a lesson in loss

days later we held a phone high
when she was off at the feeder
found a single white egg
a Jordan almond in a jeweler's plush box
then two, long axes aligned,
neat as a pin

one day she landed on the lip
tiny feet tottering on the nest's edge
and we knew another soul had arrived

but it wasn't like we thought:
big bruise-purple bumps
on translucent pink skin
no down at all
no elegance about it
it was the naked need of the just-arrived
helpless and vulnerable
but still asking for love

how could this small alien thing
so fragile and awkward
survive in a world of nos?
but she did. as did her twin –
two small, improbable yeses
weathering even the hardest hail

oh, the anticipation
as the oldest beat her wings in the nest
building strength
trying freedom
ready to launch
into a lifetime of thousand-mile journeys
almost weightless with hope

Tell Me
Julie Cadwallader Staub

Blackpoll, cerulean, mourning, magnolia,
how do you lift your wings, leave your nest,
your destination an ocean away,
the moon and salt air for company?

Blackpoll, cerulean, mourning, magnolia,
how do you stay the course, wingbeat by wingbeat,
wave upon wave, mile after mile,
and still, your tiny heart prevails?

Little bird, little bird
with death always so near,
teach me how to rise
teach me to persevere.

Should I Care

Pamela Norton Reed

Why should I care
  for this little yellow bird?
Smaller, less colorful,
      than the bills protruding from toucan nest above
and with wings that could never block the sun
like the macaws now making their scarlet circuit

Why would I care
– or notice – this
    tiny
  yellow
    bird
when the majestic motmot sits watching me
    regal with feathered train and turquoise cap

Just a tiny
    yellow
      warbler
  with its sharp shrill chirps
Like hibiscus among anthurium:
    common
    widespread
    least concern
    [like some people I know]

Nothing exotic here. Just
    Sweet.
      Sweet.
    Sweet.

Wait.

I know you.
Don't I?
Do I?
Was it you I saw
  flitting in bramble near me,
    four thousand miles from Osa?

Did you find respite in My woods?
  pause to nest
  but not rest
  you never rest

Sweet-sweet-sweet-sweet-sweet

Was it you I heard calling at the edges of Denali,
  four thousand miles from My home?

Why don't you abide safely
  in warmth and wild?
What karmic mutation has you
  constantly moving
  constantly seeking
  noticed by few but feral felines and ravenous raptors

Yes sweet,
    sweet,
      sweet.
        Yet more.

Courageous little warbler –
  You've seen more of the world
    than those you fly above
    those who never see you or
      much of
      anything

Why should I care
  for this tiny
    warbling
      miracle ?
– Lighter than the nickels in my pocket
  or the pen with which I wrote these words in wonder –

Sweet-sweet-sweet-sweet-sweet You
look me in the eye
      as if to say:
I know you, too.
Why'd you take so long to notice?
  Were you least concerned?
      Now tell the others
    All the others
  All the other others
They might need to care

Blue Jay Lives Inside of Me
Jan Lamberg

Years are days, minutes shrinking to a moment by a story's unveiling…

a scratch, a tiny heft – two bright and beadies bore into me. Done with acorn dropping, cracking on my car's roof, a blue jay hops to my side-view mirror. We know this, how in the middle of dense forest, wild birds do not lock eyes with humans…never, say, like a wolf with a buffalo. And yet, she stares, the way Moon will peer over Pelham Lake a mile back towards the village…maybe all three of us wondering – *so how many of us are there… through these sugar maples, in the water, among the stars…?*

In the fading dusk, Blue Jay still vibrates, her plumage not lightless brown, but gray, azure & sapphire trimmed in black & cloud. She gazes down into my lap at my hand, my blue jay drawing, my jay coming to life via crest, iridescent cyan tail, stroke, line, scratch by scratch.

Darkness blends white oak lobes into hemlock fur, foliage into charcoal; I blacken my Jay's profile – eye & lashes.

Remember the Romantics mirroring the Ancients: *As above, so below – indeed,* how a wild creature & my primitive suggestion have joined in correspondence, merged via bleached paper on the border of Vermont's last deactivated nuclear plant?

She bends, then straightens back into my eyes…curiosity on fire! I can't help laughing; she's fledged, cawing, dweedling…maybe laughing, too?

For us humans, too, what does it take to ignite with such wonder and keep our fire of creation going...like blue-black is to jay,...this shared life between dusk and dawn?!

The Truth About Ruby-throats
Bill Hilton Jr.

Blurred wings humming, heart fast-thrumming,
A 20-carat emerald darts though dappled leaves.
Green back, white throat and breast,
A female hummingbird.

Watch closely, closer still.

She's snatching gnats and 'skeeters — protein to make big pecs that
power wings — all while probing blooms for sweetness, and for
energy, burned up by more probing, more snatching.

Her crop-held slurry serves as food — for half-naked hummerlings
with gaping maws, in a nest so small it seems a bump on a limb.
Adroitly built of spider silk, adorned with gray-green lichens, a
bassinet for two.

From nest edge mother coughs up brunch for twittering mouths,
then ventures out to search for lunch.

Another gemstone flashes past, this one a ruby jewel with gorget
so bright it stuns until the male turns left and all goes black — an
iridescent stunt more marvelous than magic sleights-of-hand, tech-
nicolor trickery to woo a mate but hide with ease from rival eyes.

The male perches, not guarding nest and progeny but set to drive
out other males who want his flower bounty. Then zip! He's after
one more female for his harem. A frantic chase and high dive prove
his worth, his stamina, his genes. A quick cloacal kiss, his job is
done 'til that next emerald saunters by.

Summer lazes on as hummer chicks built of bugs and sugar grow, then bail from home – flight-worthy, soon to learn what's good and tasty. But days grow short, triggering a journey south toward warmer climes where insects buzz and plants still blossom. A thousand-miles or fifteen-hundred, sans map and GPS, for fledglings a route never flown but so deeply felt they end up where they're going. For old hummers, a return to winter range.

Flying the Gulf at wavetop height or in the curl most make it through but many don't, lost to wrong-way wind or running out of gas: Hors d'oeuvres for Barracuda.

Survivors – feathered expats – frolic in the balm, ticos and ticas for a time, snacking at their leisure on fruit flies and whatever sweetness erupts – a Costa Rican paradise for half the year.

The calendar advances. March days pass in Guanacaste hills until the equinox; it's spring back home in Carolina. Eat fast, fatten up, head due north – 20 hours skimming waves again, non-stop; four million heartbeats, wingbeats a million more. Impossible, they do it, with pea-sized brains so keen they end up where they started: Same town, same yard, same tree, same feeder, same as six months prior.

Impossible, indeed.

And so it goes, year-to-year, one-by-one, to-and-fro – a pilgrimage of ruby-throats toward Neotropic sites, and back again, to us. Are they ours ... or theirs? Across two continents these hummingbirds we share, but do we care? We'd better, on *both* ends of the route.

Emerald and ruby. I'd hate to lose these family jewels.

The Ovenbird (What to Learn)
Jamie K. Reaser

The ovenbird flew, lost of course, into my large window. How a tiny warbler can make such a bang is uncertain. Had it seen sky? Had it seen forest? Did it believe, with confidence, in illusions? Was it moving through the air in joy, or terror? I looked for a sharp-shinned hawk but didn't see one. I beat the local cats to it. Not broken, but battered, its little heart needing to find its way back to body and right rhythm.

Some scholars say that Robert Frost knew the ovenbird as himself. In its singing, in his verse, it learned not to sing. The Oven Bird is the poet's sonnet, true, but also an apprenticeship to the craft of surrender. Masters don't execute mastery, they give themselves over to the unmasterable. They are the diminished thing.

The ovenbird is a creature of the forest floor, a keeper of spent leaves. Leaves are camouflage. Leaves are name-sake nest. Leaves hide insects and thus must be lifted and sorted and restrewn for another day. The ovenbird knows humus as the root of humility. We, too, are of this root. Though, we forget.

"Teacher, teacher, teacher!" cries out the ovenbird when he returns each spring from his southern winter haunts. What teacher and what learning? I wonder if the ovenbird is most honest and most brilliant of us all. What would it be like to live as if every answer was insufficient? I'm considering if it is.

I became the momentary perch, my long fingers held in the curve of tiny feet and the newness of relationship. I felt the grip of nameless infants. We are all beginners, aren't we?

Snowy Owl in Queens
David Taylor

She stood out like an arctic moon
against this typical New York scene
of concrete cold and pissed off drivers,
a mass of white with dark bars against a gray sky,
high up above the roadway,
brighter than the winter.

I knew her by her size,
resting there on the street lamp,
traffic reeling by on the Belt Parkway,
a guy at the corner flipping off random drivers,
as she looked off to the south toward Jamaica Bay.

I craned my neck
and slowed my car as best I could,
as if to stretch time to see her there,
in   and   above
this city scene and the bay to the south,
a shock of snowy owl and place,
my turn of attention.

Oriolus
James Searl

In the midst of my meanderings
I stumbled on a song
Ready for the last drop
having just given up hope
Friendship called my name

And listening in I really felt
For the first time
Ever

My ears
Which calls went unheard?
How many messages have gone missed?

What's this reel?
That's the hook
chatter going back and fro
I had never noticed

Was this always the key?
I heard bars
they multiply
Quite the golden melody

So I'd never heard a bird
Like that
In that way
Before orioles

What an ancient magic I had lost

But they didn't
They never did

Wings pointed tails round
The sound finds you

If you listen

And if you want to know
You can
From Elkhart to El Salvador
They'll be singing

sweet songs

Of melodies pure and true

Snow Goose Migration
Pamela Uschuk

Iris-eyed dawn and the slow blind buffalo of fog
shoulders along flat turned fields.
We hear the bassoon a capella
before air stutters
                              to the quake that wheels.

The thermonuclear flash of snow geese,
                huge white confetti,
                              storm and tor of black-tipped wings
                                      across Shasta's silk peak,
                                            the bulging gibbous moon.

There are thousands.   Now
            no stutter but ululations
                    striking us like the riot of white water.
Wave on wave breaks
            over us. V
                    after V interlock, weave
                            like tango dancers to dip and rise
                                    as their voices hammer
silver jewelry in our hearts, our minds. These rare multitudes
            drown every sound, stop
                    every twenty-first century complaint.

Snow geese unform us.
Fluid our hands, our arms, our legs,
                our hearts. What more do we ever need

than these songs
                        cold and pure as Arctic-bladed warriors
                            circling the lake's mercuric eye?

Snake graceful above the curve of earth, snow geese wail
          through sunrise like tribal women
                into funeral flames.

Sun rouges their feathers
     as they rise
                    hossanahward, dragging us
stunned by the alchemy of their clamour.

And we long for
how it must have been each season
for millenia while Modocs harvested wild rice
     blessed by the plenty of wings
       over the plenty of water
before slaughter moved in with the settlers.
The few Modoc survivors were exiled to Oklahoma
to make way for potato farms
     that even now poison the soil
and drain Tule Lake.

In the month of wild plum blossoms, we would pretend
it is the early world.
       Snow geese migrate through sky wide
as memory. Their wild choirs lift us
       beyond the dischords of smoking fields and tractors
to light struck ice white, to our own forgotten wings
              and ungovernable shine.

Birds on Mars
Geoffrey Garver

As I lay on the picnic table in the surprise of a rest area nestled between farms along the gravel road between St-Eugène-de-Ladrière and Trois-Pistoles, watching and waiting for meteors to flash through the mid-August night sky, I am happy to be out of ear shot of the *autodrome* where the metallic screech of stock cars delights some and dismays others on summer Saturday nights in St-Eugène-de-Ladrière, a quiet Québec dairy town in Bas-St-Laurent, and town is a big word for it, and quiet doesn't include Saturday night. The Airbnb listing mentioned the dairy farms and the short distance to *Parc National du Bic* which I love and (the clincher) that dogs are welcome but, yeah, not the *autodrome*. If a common nighthawk were out catching bugs I could hear him as I swim my eyes all over the sky to see more than I can really see at once. I look and listen and no nighthawk but there goes a barred owl's who-cooks-for you, and one glorious streak of a shooting star delights me in the minutes I lie there, and I also have time during my impatience for the Perseids to ask myself as I gaze skyward if there will be birds on Mars after all those crazy folks move there, and come to think of it why is it taking them so long. Will they and will there be? I'm thinking probably no birds, yeah, definitely not any birds, but chances are good for an *autodrome*.

Baltimore Oriole; Aqui y Allí (Here And There)
David Taylor

In the old part of Havana, near the *Floridita*,
where the tourists line up on the sidewalk for a daiquiri and a table inside,
I saw a Baltimore oriole darting between the buildings,
making its way to *Parque Central*.

A street musician sang *Guantanamera* on the corner,
his hat in front of him with a few coins inside.
The oriole found fruit left out on the balconies,
his brief flute notes now and then

Aqui y allí (here and there) I thought.
I was returning to Long Island tomorrow,
back to an icy January. He'd return in July
and find the orange halves I hang from the trees.

I am an honest man/From where the palm tree grows,
the musician sang. I'm an honest man too
I said to myself and laughed a little
at my cursory Spanish, the oriole rounding the corner.

Here and there, there and here.
Every *there* has a *here* in it.
Every season is also a place.
The oriole here and the oriole there.
Flip a coin. One side, two.

Merced Wildlife Sanctuary
Tanvi Dutta Gupta

It may be only one red-tailed hawk darting a foil too close, yet the snow geese sense danger and rise. Looking through my binoculars, my eyes blind with their white thrumming mass – cloud-like – birds made weather made bird once more. We hear them even from several hundred wingspans away: a symphony of percussive windbeat and trebled birdsong that swells and sinks and swells once more with the geese, who seem, as one feathered form, to search for something together, the edges of the cumulous mass brushing the ground, and then rising upwards once more.

Whatever it is, they don't find it: seconds later they have rained downwards and settled the sky back to doldrums blue.

"I wonder if we'll see that in thirty years," someone says.

"I wonder if we'll see that in ten," I say, the cynicism too familiar to sting: after all, everywhere this world burns as climate change unsettles every bedrock and ecosystems crumble – down swing – without memorial. I can't differ most days between learning and mourning.

We drive away. I look back to where a smaller flock has startled upwards. They smudge over the horizon line. We pass through corn rows where more geese have settled at pond edge. People planted this land for birds, not wanting them to raid the fields of farmers around, and so the geese keep returning for these weeks, year on year, to gloss the ground in a great brief storm.

Rhyme of the Modern Mariner
Carl Safina

There lives a bird, the Albatross
Who sails the ocean foam.
The greatest wand'rer of all time
No land do they call home.
Instead, the Albatross lives life
Remote from coast and shore,
It flies a thousand-thousand miles,
And then – it flies some more.

It captures the propelling wind
Like ships over the sea.
Then robs the gales for weightlessness,
inverting gravity.
With wings as wide as two tall men
The ocean's breadth it bests
Yet faithfully returns to light
Upon its precious nest.

On their great wings these sturdy things
thus glide so far and wide,
They've skimmed the seas a million years
But may not stem the tide
Of people who both love the sea
Yet love the sea too much –
Our appetites unknowingly
The Albatross do touch

It's true, this soul called Albatross
Who sails the ocean yet
Must cope with modern mariners
With fishing hook and net.

To have our fish – and eat them too –
Requires but a thought,
Yet so unthinking have we been
That albatross gets caught.

Where wanders thou, oh albatross?
Wilst vanish from the deep?
Or will we mend our ways in time
Your flight with us to keep?
Have patience with us, albatross,
Our malice isn't meant.
And if we lose you for all time
We'll claim, "An accident!"
But if that comes to pass, who'll suffer? –
You? Or we? Or both?
I'll offer this: it's **we** who'll miss
Your grace behind our boat.

Do Pine Siskins Not See Color?
Whit Gibbons

In winter, as always, they come
in mixed and unmixed flocks, seeking a place
to settle and feed: northern cardinals, blue jays,
yellow-rumped warblers – some permanent residents,

some migrants, back every year to these Carolina woods.
Landing on the deck rail, the tufted titmice and Carolina chickadees
and American goldfinches feed comfortably on sunflower seeds
in their plenty, scattered along the railing by an oft-seen hand.

Some choose suet, nailed to the white oak: the woodpeckers,
red-bellied and downy, and the white-breasted nuthatch.
The solitary ones, the self-contained units. They fly in, and back
to a branch, and in again – each one taking its turn.

The meal worms have their own best customers:
American robins, Carolina wrens, gray catbirds.
Some offer hints of early pairings –
a flashing thought of spring, nest sites to be selected.

In the trees, colors flutter like flags of countries
recently visited by some on their long travels.
A yellow-bellied sapsucker's headdress sports Mexico's red.
A blue-headed vireo wears Belize's blue.

I watch from the cabin's screened-in porch
as a small flock of pine siskins, drawn to the array of seeds,
swoops down from the trees to the deck.
They land all together, in a wave, like water tossed from a bucket.

Their heads are bent to the serious work of eating.

The flecks of darker brown against their lighter plumage
look like dashed and dotted lines
running the length of their small selves. And their selves

are all together, brown and buff and splashes of yellow.
But one is not like the others.
Still a siskin, yet not brown with yellowish wings.
This one is ivory white.

Yet side by side, they gather seeds, a pleasing sight.
They fly in a cohesive flock, again
and again, into the trees. And again
they return to the railing, white and brown,

landing all together. Albino? Leucistic?
A geneticist might know. Anyway,
I applaud pine siskins not seeing color,
not minding, when one is not like the others.

Mississippi Kite, Late Summer
Hope Coulter

Cut like an airplane die against pale blue, the kite glides
in great, relaxed loops – all movement, and all motionless

but for the tilting, now and again, of wing or tail, each crook
an adjustment, redirecting the body against the current:

the speed somehow nonchalant, like how a skater pours forward
in long bending strokes with his hands clasped behind his back,

or a swimmer shoots off from the wall, then stills her arms
and lets momentum propel her, simply to feel the water,

each clear bubble streaming past. Between the bird and me
a fringe of pine needles, the fleece of crêpe myrtle blossoms –

in my ears a tinny song:

> *My country's skies are bluer than the ocean*
> *and sunlight gleams on cloverleaf and pine –*

A banking, an easy drop. Stall and ascent. This flight is relaxed,
inscribing arcs that slow my own breath in the tracking.

> *But other lands have sunlight too, and clover…*

Higher and higher the bird tacks, lazily, never betraying the urge of lift
beneath its wings. One of these times it won't descend again –

off to the other America, crossing invisible borders.
For now, still tethered to the groundward loop.

Wheel Turning on the Hub of the Sun
William Pitt Root

I was young.
                A hundred yards off at the edge of the reflective
        mud
tall birds white like spirits gathered for a ceremonial
dance stalked slowly along the bottom
as the surface of the pond gave back the dance.
Each strode in the pool of its own image
and the queer noises they made
made the silence deeper.

The sun was a member of their dance and the trees
lent shadows to the edges of the pond shimmering
like water in a saucer tipped.

What I can remember now
comes as from a dream glowing in the mind until it's
spoken of, and goes away. I know
that they strode in their dance for hours
and drew their long yellow legs up into the commotion of
        their wings
and rose in a great circle overhead, their wheel
above me turning on the hub of the sun,
– and that when they were gone, standing like one
in a darkness after lightning
in the light that once had seemed sufficient,
I found myself alone.

Bye-bye
Derek Sheffield

The animal of winter is dying,
its white body everywhere
in collapse and stabbed at
by straws of light, a leaving
to believe in as the air
slowly fills with darkness
and water drains from the tub
where my daughter, watching it
lower around her, feeling it
go, says about the only thing
she can as if it were a long-
kept breath going with her
blessing of dribble and fleck.
Down it swirls a living drill
vanishing toward a land
where tomorrow already
fixes its bright eye on a man
muttering his way into a crowd,
saying about the only thing
he can before his body
goes *boom*. And tomorrow,
I will count more dark shapes
tumbling from the sky, birds
returning to scarcity, offering
in their see-sawing songs
a kind of liquidity.

TO LAMENT

Swallows, Falling
Kathleen Dean Moore

I.

Hundreds of swallows are flying over the river that flows alongside the sandstone cliff. On out-stretched wings, they fall through rising columns of air and ride their momentum back into the sky, as if each swings on a trapeze of taut spider silk, up and up to that breathless still point, and then down and down. A banking turn through clouds of midges, a steep dive toward a damselfly, then a swallow hurtles toward her nest with a mouthful of legs.

II.

Two swallows ascend into the sky above the cliff, stall, and fall together. As they fall, they flutter their wings to descend in a close spiral, their bodies repeatedly coming together with the lightest touch. Here is the heart-stopping plunge down the sandstone layers, down past the brown line that marks the Cretaceous extinction, down past the orange band populated with the wing-bones of pterosaurs, past the thick line of the Permian extinction – this dance of falling – down past the white stratum encasing the calcified shells of sea lilies, down and down. And just as they touch the shadow over the water, they spread their wings and sail back into the hot noon of this day.

III.

In mid-summer, when their nests are empty and silent, their fledglings flown, swallows begin to fly south. They don't fatten up before they leave. They will feed on the wing. In large flocks, maybe two hundred, maybe more, the swallows will make their way through Central America to buzzing fields and marshes in Brazil, Uruguay, Argentina, flying and feeding in the daylight, resting at night.

IV.

On August 2, 2020, swallows began to fall out of the sky. First in northern New Mexico and then all across the state and into Texas. Not just swallows, but warblers and flycatchers too. People saw them fall. A bird's flapping wings slowed, stalled. A moment of stillness and the bird nose-dived into the dust. Not just a bird. Thousands of birds. Hundreds of thousands. Where people might have found 2 or 3 dead birds a year, there were 20 in one front yard, 300 along a river. *Southwest Avian Mortality*: the website tried to record them all, but there was no counting. Look up the photos. There they are in tight rows, lying on their backs on a table, their legs drawn up, their claws curled closed, their eyes gone white and blind.

The dead birds weighed almost nothing, scientists said. Skin and bones, that's all. Starving, they ate themselves up. That was the summer that wildfires tore through the coastal forests, crackling under thunderclouds of smoke, and the birds turned fatally inland, into the Chihuahuan desert. There was sun in the desert sky. But no moisture. And no insects.

V.

Falling. Falling out of the sky – in North America, a drop of 3 billion birds in fifty years – poisoned maybe, starved, some of them, lying dead at the base of skyscrapers or wind turbines, lying dead where cats left them on the welcome mats, dying with eggs in their bellies and no place to build a nest, their songs drowned, their wings broken. A swallow is a tiny thing – it weighs no more than eight pennies. But over 150 million years, it has learned to sail on the sky. When the last swallow plunges to Earth, surely the sky also will fall.

A Sign of Life
Geoffrey Garver

Maybe on this crisp March morning
A year to the day since your long life ceased
You will give me a sign,

I said in my head or aloud,
Who knows?
I was alone.

A sign,
Or maybe your still presence
Will be enough. It has been.

This special place was yours
And ours. You mothered it and me
In countless ways.

The fieldstone fireplace
Warmed your waning days.
As you wished.

The well-worn kitchen
You no longer commanded.
Like your garden it is in other hands.

But you are everywhere here.
In books and photos
And long walks in the woods.

A wood duck or two did not always
Grace the pond
When you arrived for your morning swim.

Not in early March
When you sat bundled and still on the pond facing bench
In wonder. But sometimes.

Today I pass the pond
And enter the neighbor's woods
Where chanterelles grow,

Where wild leek blanket the ground in May,
Where vireos and woodpeckers
Occupy their seasons.

I come to the wild meadow
That in your lifetime
Slowly grew and took on new life.

When did the blue-winged warblers
Start nesting here?
Before I knew, I'm sure.

No warblers now, no buntings.
I might surprise a grouse
Or find turkey tracks in the fading snow.

Above, a faint cry.
Two great blue herons
Grace the sky.

No, not herons.
Sandhill cranes,
Crimson heads pointing north.

This place you taught me
To know and love
Is blessed with birdlife,

And now these graceful cranes
Greet me here the first time ever.
A sign in the stillness.

Hermit Thrush
Walker Abel

To stand in the intimate orb of its song
threads of well-being weave into stillness

And I wish it a spell so powerful
that fifty years I might suspend and dwell

Not asleep, but fully awake to the music
that flutes like tendrils of mist through forest

A spell suffusing its chamber of sound
with assurance that all things are surpassingly well

And when coming to move again I'd wish
for an earth not dire or overheated

For people still enamored of the spell
where thrush and human in concert dwell.

Arctic
William Pitt Root

From its polished display case
this one stares back at us,
almost contemptuous.

Dead claws hooked
in the lifelike branch,
its beak is half parted
as if to remark
on the brass
of the nameplate
where Greco-Latin nominations
encase him in another
kind of glass
to be held back by,
beheld in.
          No wind
will alert him
of our penance.
No snapped branch
set him
soaring like a moon
among glazed clouds.
Nor will the museum's
rats tempt him
in the dark
to hunch and spread
his wings and tail and fall
silent as moonlight
upon the quick hot
frenzy in the fur.

Nor in fact
could anything be said
to move him now.
This is what we learn
from him, if
we learn at all: That he
is dead, stuffed
among the mystery
of all he has been.
Is changed as we
are changed,
gazing upon him.

Moon-eyed Owl,
for whom the night is eyes,
cloud-voiced Owl,
charged by the intelligence
of snow to utter brilliance,
it is you, Lightning-taloned,
you of the arrow-tongue,
you alone who know how to summon
from live red flesh that breath
bright as dew called from grasses by the sun.

And it is you, Whose-Feathers-Whisper
you of whom it is known
that we will
hear him
one day, or one night,
hear him call our name
in a language of light
that must illuminate us
each in the locked museum

of all we thought
we knew and, having heard,
we will rise up
nearer to voice
on our unfathomable wings
to ask who he was calling for, who? Who?

Ri Elaq'omab'

Apab'yan Tew (English Translation, Jamie K. Reaser)

¡Elaq'om, elaq'om!
¡Elaq'om, elaq'omab'!

Allí van los ladrones, allí van sembrando las nubes, van dejando la semilla que será tormenta, después de ocultar al sol. "Allí van los ladrones," repito y canto mientras mi tía abuela me mira con alegría.

There the thieves go, there they sow the clouds, they leave the seed that will be a storm, after they occlude the sun. "There go the thieves," I repeat and sing while my great-aunt looks at me with joy.

"Este año han llegado muchos y uno que otro despistado, que vuela solitario aquí y allá", explica mi tía abuela, Talin. "Primero pasa el viento y el viento les abre el camino en el bosque, cuando los árboles quedan sin hojas, entonces los ladrones tienen donde descansar. Siempre escogen el monte alto, en esa parte donde a la lluvia le da por esconderse."

"This year many have arrived and one or another clueless, flying alone here and there," explains my great-aunt, Talin. "First the wind passes and the wind opens the way for them in the forest, when the trees are without leaves, then the thieves have a place to rest. They always choose the high mountain, in that part where it is possible for the rain to hide."

La noche queda en silencio y la luna se asoma, las estrellas y los ladrones cruzan sus caminos, formando una cruz. Cuando el último ladrón pasa, entonces puedes levantarte más temprano, recibes a la estrella de la mañana y escuchas cómo los ladrones se ponen de acuerdo con el sol que regresa. Entre ellos se entienden.

The night is silent and the moon rises, the stars and the thieves cross their paths, forming a cross. When the last thief passes, then you can get up earlier, greet the morning star and listen to the thieves agree with the returning sun. They understand each other.

Y entonces se van. No toman nada, solo se van.

And then they go. They don't take anything, they just leave.

"Talin, ¿por qué les decimos ladrones si no toman nada?"

"Talin, why do we call them thieves if they don't take anything?"

"Porque se llevan el tiempo. Desde el día que aparecen, ya no hay descanso. Hay que afilar el machete y conseguir un nuevo sombrero. El último trueno está cerca y los campos de maíz te esperan. ¡Ah! y también, por supuesto, por el antifaz que usan en sus ojos."

"Because they rob you of time. From the day they appear, there is no rest. You have to sharpen the machete and get a new hat. The last thunder is near and the cornfields await you. Oh! and also, of course, because of the mask they wear on their eyes."

Notas:
Elaq'om: ladrón en idioma k'iche' del altiplano central de Guatemala. Ladrones, ladrón: referente a la migración del halcón peregrino.

Notes:
Elaq'om: means thief in the K'iche' language from the central highlands of Guatemala. Ladrones, ladrón: refers to the migration of the peregrine falcon.

To the Swainson's Thrush
Erin Robertson

the hard thwack at the window
was gentler than seeing your stunned form
still on the ground
legs angled to sky
streaked cream breast heaving
head tilted, panting

the worst bit was you were alive
it ought to have been a fierce enough blow
to let you pass without knowing
or feeling the end

if only you'd gone out
winging your way through birches
barely sensing the pain
and finality of the end

that's what I thought
of my grandfather's stroke –
a pity he'd lived
to learn what life could take away

we offered meager comfort
stroking your feathers
speaking in whispers
keeping your bloodied eye
an unspoken secret among us

your breaths dwindled
eyelids blinked slowly
closed longer each time

then came the stillness
of the absence of soul –
something undeniable
I first felt when
our first dog died -
from breath to no breath
in the slightest flicker of time

Migrante (Migrant)
Rafael Calderón-Parra

Ya se caen las hojas,
El otoño ya llegó,
Yo te espero muy ansioso,
De ese viaje agotador.

The leaves are already falling,
Autumn has arrived,
I wait for you very anxiously,
From that tiring journey.

De tierras lejanas,
Desde el norte viajarás,
Por desiertos y montañas,
Y a veces, incluso el mar.

From distant lands,
From the north you will travel,
Through deserts and mountains,
And sometimes, even the sea.

No existen fronteras,
Para ti, todo es hogar,
Pero pasa, que no encuentras,
Las cosas, en su lugar.

There are no borders,
For you, everywhere is home,
But it happens, you can't find,
The things in their place.

Del, bosque que amabas,
Queda solo un árbol ya,
Ese lago de aguas claras,
Hoy es negro, cual pesar.

From the forest you loved,
There is only one tree left
That lake of clear waters,
Today is black, like grief.

Sé que te he fallado,
Protegiendo nuestro hogar,
He dejado que el concreto,
Cubra lo que amamos más.

I know I've failed you
protecting our home
I've let the concrete
Cover what we love most.

Tú, que eres migrante,
Tú bien sabes del dolor,
Encontrar, que a tu regreso,
Lo que amaste, se esfumó.

You, who are a migrant,
You know well the pain
Finding that upon your return,
What you loved is gone.

Al menos te ofrezco,
Un remanso, una canción,
El jardín del cual soy dueño,
Para ti, lo planté yo.

At least I offer you
A haven, a song,
The garden I own,
For you, I planted it.

Cuando digo "a ti", es "a ustedes",
Que a mi invierno traen color,
Con sus plumas me cambiaron,
Aves migratorias, son.

When I say "for you," I mean "for all of you,"
Who bring color to my winter,
With your feathers you changed me,
Migratory birds, are.

Great Blue
Pamela Norton Reed

On the last morning of my first week of being alive, I walked to the edge of the earth and loitered there. Toes straddled the foamy oscillations of the line dividing sand from sea. Or sea from sand. And the third axis was sky. The ocean called so loudly I heard only its deafening silence punctuated by the rhythmic crash of the soft cobalt marbles catapulted onto shore by sirens and mermen. Women of war to walk among.

On the last morning of my first week of feeling alive, I walked the edge of the earth, determined to brand the essence of forgiveness and freedom into my heart while rising sun caressed my shoulders. Sand became rock. Fearful had become fearless as the now alive me found routes through the crags.

He caught me unawares, further out on the edge of the earth. Guard, or guardian. He stood posing, in profile, bracing against wind and wave. Great. Blue. Great blue here. In my nearly gone first week of living, there he stood. Sentry, or sentinel. It was his presence, I know, that caused my arms to reach to the sky and my lungs to exclaim "Yes-Yes" to the universe or to the heron or to the wind or to me. Yes. Yes. If this heron can be here, alive, fighting the elements, I can fly home, and stay alive, fighting my elements. Great blue. Message, or messenger.

And to this day of staying alive, I do not know if it was a heron, or my father.

Western Tanager
Pamela Uschuk

Back from hiking the far mountains, I find
your desiccated body perfect, black wings
tucked under the slick yellow back,
orange head intact but for eyes eaten by sky.

Slim sarcophagus you bear no wounds.
Neither owl, cat nor hawk tried to eat you.
Your petrified beak cocks its last song
to the invisible sea beyond Sombero Peak. Sleek,
your mummified carcass offers no clues.
Were you smashed to earth by monsoon or
did our picture window lure you to secure
branches growing in glass?

Beauty, I can't bury you, won't disturb your solemn rest
on the picnic table among presidential lies
in the *New York Times*, bellowing his urgent need
to build a twenty-foot-high steel wall to secure our border
from unarmed refugees. You nestle with turret shells
from the Sea of Cortez, a sand dollar said to
contain the crucifixion, lovely beyond belief.

Lithe acrobat
          too rarely have I seen you flip
through memory's eucalyptus leaves.
          Where do you sing?
                    A full moon collapses

like the Halloween pumpkin on the porch.
I gentle you weightless to my shelf.
Time never rests,
        its ghost prints leading us over a horizon giddy
                        with insistent light
we cannot conceive will ever end.

Common Murre
Kathleen Dean Moore

Wearing a yellow raincoat, a boy wandered the beach between the high-tide line and the falling tide. He leaned over now and then to drop a treasure into his blue bucket. The little boy was whistling. Whenever he is content, he is whistling. The sandpipers piped. A gull threw back her head and brayed. The bell-buoy chimed. I sat on a drift-log, grinning, as the voices came together to shake the air into something lovely and pure.

The boy suddenly paused and took a few steps backward. His whistling stopped. With his plastic shovel, the boy dug at a disheveled black form, matted in blown sand. It took him several tries to pry it into his bucket. I went to him as he turned toward me. What he had in his bucket was the limp body of a black-and-white sea bird, a common murre.

Murres have always been one of the most numerous of marine birds – maybe 13 to 24 million at their peak. But now, in the warming, souring ocean, they are struggling to find the fish they need to feed their chicks and keep themselves alive. I had hoped it would be a long time before the great starving would reach the Oregon coast, but this might be the beginning of it, in this blue bucket.

I did not talk to the boy about this. Carefully, we emptied the bucket onto a polished log. Here was the body of the murre, feathers broken, head hanging. Here was a blue by-the-wind sailor, a small jellyfish with a wing to catch the wind. Here was a mudstone, shaped by the fossilized shell of an ancient butter clam.

The murre would want to be buried here, at the beach, the boy decided – in the place it knows and loves best, where its mom and dad are probably nearby, looking for him. So this is what we did. We dug a hole behind the log, buried the murre in sand, and decorated the grave with the treasures the boy had found. Standing erect, looking out to sea, the boy whistled a sad song for the dead bird. Then, hand-in-hand, we walked back down the beach under the terrible silence of the empty sky.

Lonely Sky
Paul A. Riss

I've been looking up since I was a boy
There are less now but I keep looking
I'll never stop trying to find them
I'll spend all my days searching
They have to be somewhere

The sky isn't what it used to be
It was always so full
Now there's much less to see
A sky without them is only blue
A sky without them is only grey
A sky without them is nothing but clouds

It hasn't always been this way
In my past I've seen so many
Now all I see up there is blue
Clear skies is our normal
Where has my happiness gone

The sky isn't what it used to be
It was always so full
Now there's so much less to see
A sky without them is only blue
A sky without them is only grey
A sky without them is nothing but clouds

In my youth you crisscrossed the air
My memories are flashed with colour
This reality doesn't seem fair
I will not accept you're gone
I will not spend my days looking down

The sky isn't what it used to be
It was always so full
Now there's so much less to see
A sky without them is only blue
A sky without them is only grey
A sky without them is nothing but clouds

A sky without them is only blue
A sky without them is only grey
A sky without them is nothing but lonely

Mother Canada Goose
April Tierney

During spring, Canada geese fly northward
in their great V's above the Colorado Rockies.
The bowed shape of prayer is all but useless
to us at this time of year – we throw our heads
and hearts back instead, looking up to behold them –
a skein of benediction soaring across our western sky.

Invariably, one loyal pair always stops to nest
at the algae covered pond in my rural neighborhood.
A few years ago I saw the mother goose scouting
out that sanctified place where she would eventually
create refuge for her young. She stood atop a big boulder
on the hill above our house, calling out, claiming
her part in the profound story unfurling before us.

The day I saw her I was eight months pregnant,
waddling along with equal parts awe and apprehension.
She stood strong and proud on the very same boulder
that I sat in front of one year prior while fasting and praying
for a vision – three long days and nights out on the land
audaciously asking the world if I was meant to become
a mother. I wrestled with this question for a long time

fearing for the mess that future generations would inherit,
wondering if it was wise or kind to bring more life
onto this broken and overpopulated planet.
When I finally decided to go up onto the mountain,
I promised my husband that I would say yes
to whatever answer came faithfully through the trees,
the bees, the wind, the rocks, and the rain.

So on that third day when I saw the face of our future child
emerge from the same boulder that this mother goose
now stands upon after flying hundreds of miles
to find her nest, I knew my bones were fiercely blessed.

But I also wondered, did the goose ever question if this
changing world would be viable enough to support her young?
Did fear or doubt ever enter her hollow-boned body,
haunt her dreams, alter her patterns of flight?

I do not know the answers to these questions
but I do know that she chose the pond carefully,
that she found someplace quiet and kind
for her five downy goslings to grow into robust
and brave birds so that they could make
their mighty journey south come winter.

I know that our children grew
into the world alongside one other.
I know that she and I are life bearers
and that without us, there is no story
to tell. I know that when her family
eventually flew from the pond,
I missed them terribly

and that my daughter will hear tales
about their elegance and intelligence
for as long as there is wind in my lungs.

Solace of Swallows
Gwendolyn Morgan

The violet-green, barn and cliff swallows
return from Goya, Argentina, from Carara, Costa Rica
from San Juan Capistrano to build and rebuild

their nests of mud from Chicken Creek,
with wild grasses, and small leaves from maple trees
cemented under the eaves of her house.

Only one pair of cliff swallows this year, she says.
She remembers hundreds, clouds of swallows
returning when she was a child

white droppings along the porch
like letters on the chalkboard
petroglyphs of ancestral birds.

This morning she draws outlines of children
who have been killed in gun violence,
during border crossings, white chalk on cement.

The swallows circle overhead, a sweet call in B-flat;
they carry our hearts with them.

Vacillations/Flycatcher Lament

Kim Schnuelle

Each year, we are less
until soon
we may be only a hole in the sky
the size of a broken heart.

Once, southwest willow flycatchers
rounded alders and Salix
in a cacophony of dawn song,
and shaded the air
dry olive in considered passing
above cedar, cholla, and cypress:
A tyranny of flyers
on southern pilgrimage.

Entrained down ancestral paths,
We were legion.
Had my forebears
dropped ribbons of black velvet
under their fall migrations,
would the land be marked still?
Would schoolgirls twist these remnants
band tight into pigtail bows
and hallow our names in verse?
Would we abide well known
in farmhouse, field, and imagination?

For now such streamers
would be a weak braid indeed.
Plaited in erratic arcs,
following the beaked grab

of gnats, hornets, and winged ants.
Our flight a mere thread,
so tenuous in its breaking.

And if we are then vanished,
if the memory of our traces, our barred wings
snaps, like boughs in snowfall,
who will sing our tribute?
Will we be chorus-joined in lamenting
the Carolina parakeets,
Bachman's warblers,
seaside sparrows
all gone before us?
Or will we fall alone,
a tindered pyre
banished in our demise?

This fortune's wavering
lingers over silent ponds,
tamarisk-choked runnels.
Yet our thread holds still
as a wild summoning,
a feral invocation.
A poem
to those who yet feel
our hearts pulsing and vibrant
above in fall's darkening skies.

The Least Tern
Emily Polk

On the same day three police officers pinned Mario Gonzalez
face down in the mulch
And watched as he drew his last breath
in a park right down the street from my house,
dozens of least terns returned to the six-mile island where I live.
Flying right over his body, the long-endangered birds arrived
    in Alameda,
where they have built one of their most productive breeding
    colonies in the world.
At only nine inches long with a wingspan of nearly 20 inches,
the smallest member of the gull family flies more than 3,000 miles
from Central and South America every spring to get to our
    urban island.

The least tern's miraculous arrival every spring is highly anticipated.
The "Return of the Terns" is a popular annual event
Hundreds of locals attend a least tern natural history program
And $10 gets you a seat on a bus that takes you right into
the gated area where their nests are kept safe and protected.

Mario was 26 years old the morning he died.
He lived with his four-year-old son, his mother,
and his 23-year-old brother with autism, in deep East Oakland
and he took care of all of them.
                    (HE TOOK CARE OF ALL OF THEM)
The pandemic hit him hard. He lost his job.
He struggled with anxiety from other losses.
He worried all the time about his family.

The least terns' gray backs, white underbellies and deep wing beat
sometimes cause people to mistake them for butterflies.

Adults have a sharp white triangle above their bright yellow beak
    and a black cap.
Sometimes they are called "sea sparrows" because they are so little,
but the nickname does not do justice to their vulnerability or
    their risk of extinction.

The small park where Mario was murdered used to be called
    Scout Park
At just half an acre, it is one of the smallest parks on the island,
right across the street from the South Shore shopping center.
I have walked past this park a thousand times.
Its handful of benches and green grass that abut the lagoon
was made with the help of the Navy and dedicated to
"All scouts and scouters of Alameda, past, present and in the future."

When the endangered birds were discovered in the 1970s
at the now-closed Naval Air Station,
the Navy placed logs around their nesting area on the airfield.
A seasonal monitor was hired to ensure their safety.
Their efforts landed them national praise on the news.

Mario was just three months old when his mother
took the same migratory path of the least terns
to immigrate to California from Mexico.
Like so many before her, she wanted to survive.
                    She wanted her babies to survive.

A man who said he lived next to Scout Park called 911
on the morning he saw Mario sitting on a bench
with two opened bottles of alcohol at his feet.
Mario wasn't "doing anything wrong," he told the 911 operator
"He's just scaring my wife."

Down the street, I was getting ready for work
my children tucked safe in their beds,
their faces flushed with dreams.
When they woke we talked neither of birds, nor men
But about summer coming soon,
the world opening up again.

Mario spoke calmly with police at first.
They requested his identification, which he did not or could not
    produce.
"Please put your hand behind your back," they said. "Please stop
    resisting us."
Mario did not resist, but three officers pushed him face down into
    the ground,
placing a knee on his back and holding him down with their arms.

Four minutes passed with Mario gasping for air.
"I didn't do nothing," he said. "Please don't do this."
He apologized to the police officers.
He asked for forgiveness.
He lost consciousness.
Officers rolled him over, performed CPR and delivered Narcan.
It was no use.
He was dead.

The least tern is still endangered and vulnerable to extinction.
Development continues to cause dramatic losses to colonies.
The nests get destroyed by crowds of beachgoers.
But on this island people make sure they live.
The least terns started nesting a couple of weeks after Mario died.
The birds take to the air while they are courting in what has been
    described
by one local bird expert as,

"tiny blue angels doing the tango without the roaring engines."
The tango is as much about mating as it is a celebration of life.
"We are still here," their avian dance calls over the bay.
"We have made it this far! Now we will make more of us!"

The least tern's voice is high pitched and sweet,
unlike other terns or gulls.
You can hear their birdsong in the summers
mixing with the sounds of children squealing on the island's shore.
You can even hear it in Scout Park,
above the din of traffic on Otis Avenue
it rises through the pine trees hugging the edge of the lagoon;
it rises over the patch of blood-stained grass,
over the memorials of the ones we never protected.
It rises over all the mistakes we have made,
over our grief and our desire to reimagine a world
where all living beings are cared for equally and equitably.
Every spring, the least tern returns
like a promise being kept
and every spring she sings
as though she is the only one left:

        "I survived! I survived! I survived!"

In Crepuscular Light
Rosemerry Wahtola Trommer

These warm summer evenings
I take in the nighthawks
looping above the field.
I take in their fast and agile flight,
take in their long and pointed wings.
Come winter, I will be grateful
to have stored such things.
When the nighthawks are gone
and the world is dim,
I will want to remember them –
their aerialist displays, the way
they make of the dusk a playground,
the way the whole night
seems to hang on an angling wing –
Oh summer is such a generous thing.
Even the dark is charged with the thrill
of living. Even this heart, wounded
and bruised, can't help but open
to the wheeling of nighthawks,
how they arc and sweep
as the sun disappears
and then continue their swooping
long after the light is gone.

Colonial Biogeographic Nomenclature, a Sonnet For Biological Textbooks
David George Haskell

Names that cage and capture are sick
– our books are inked with pain
Exhibit one: Neo Tropic
A term that aims to train.

Oriental? Antipodes?
Words are colonist loot
Tags whose meanings unroot and seize
and keep the "natives" mute.

Longitude centered on Greenwich
Even geography bows.
Imperial quest to enrich
Turns truths under the plow.

Enough of crude Latinized claims:
restore indigenous names.

I Am in Love with the Mourning Dove
April Tierney

I am in love with the mourning dove,
though it wasn't until recently
that I learned how to properly spell
this graceful and gray-brown
bird's poetic name.

For years I listened to their long songs
and wondered how anyone could possibly think
such choral creatures only called out in the mornings,
when their bounty wrapped its melody around me
all throughout the day. The spelling of words baffles me;

dyslexia was not something people talked about
when I was young, though there was a teacher
who told me I should simply give up on writing
because hopeless was the only way to categorize
my inability to force letters into sequences
I could not understand. And so, I stopped writing

for a long while, I stopped trying
to decipher the English language,
to make beauty bloom from branches
withered by a culture untrained in balladry.
But I never gave up on the bird's songs

there was nothing to spell in their jubilation,
their elegies, their lyrical display of artistry.
They are the original keepers of the oral tradition,
they are the storytellers, soothsayers, magic
makers – I too abide by that cosmology.

And now that I know this dove,
who's sound turns itself like a key
into the quiet hallway of my bones,

is not misnamed as the administrator of mornings
but who knows mourning as a pathway to divinity——
who laments with the rising and falling tides of
this troubled world, who grants me permission
to grieve even when grieving has gone out

of fashion. Now that I know, I can simply go on listening
to their long songs as I always have, as I always will,
as the admiring, baffled one I cannot help but be.

Eulogy for a Moving Miracle, Pts 1 & 2
Coreen Weilminster

PT I HUMMINGBIRD

Tiny jewel.
Mighty sprite.
Winged wonder.

You left your spark in my yard.

We marveled
at the miracle you are,
modified scales
masquerading
as feathers gleaming.

Animal-leaf.
Shifting light turns dull black throat
to iridescent scarlet.

My heart swelled at your magic
then ached when my daughter cried because you were so beautiful.

I cried too
for your journey cut short.
And wondered where you felt pulled to be.

Gone.

We found a mossy hollow
At the base of an old holly
and placed you there.
Instantly invisible.

Cavity made catacomb
for our majestic mini.

PT 2 REDSTART

I cannot imagine what
carries them so far.

I know all about the need to move.
The fuel to get them there.
The fronts and currents of air that "move" them
and the stars that guide them.

But what?
What compels them to stay the course
with risks in reflected sky
and house cat
and hurricane?

Why so very far, too?

That urge must be
so intense
as to consume.

She is the only redstart I saw this year.
Extraordinary
in delicate softness
and elegance
and tenacity.

A shooting star I briefly hold,
leaving a vapor of death
in my palm.

It's Just Luck
Carl Safina

A blur of gray was all I saw. So I yelled, What was *that!* Patricia
flung the door, and as gale-gusts blasted, the two of us looked
over the wooden railing *straight down* to where any angel might
have fallen and – sure enough, spread-eagled, mouth agape, a tern,
this year's young, perfect save for the fact that bad luck had put so
fierce a storm into the path of so early a youth, right at summer's
end during so crucial a transition to independence. It was a slow,
sullen storm, a real lingerer. And I looked at the water, white as
anger, and I knew: no tern could find a fish for days in this, and
that this would be particularly hard on the slender young. So when
our neighbor Eric delivered another tern, lifeless, to us, I knew
they must be dying by the hundreds in this storm. A band number
and a phone call informed me that this bright-eyed and defiant
feathered flame who had been smacked lame against our home
had, as a days-old chick, been cradled and leg-banded by Helen,
for whom I'd worked 39 years earlier and who for all these decades
has each summer bent to her mission as though gardening seabirds.
Pulling the weeds so they may nest, chasing hungry gulls so chicks
might grow, seeing it good. A few years ago she'd found two adult
terns, nesting, whom I myself – on an island 60-odd miles distant
and *twenty-five years earlier* – had plucked from their safe-haven
nest and to whom I had applied my own numbered bands to their
young legs. We were all young then. We all survived. But now this
gale was killing this year's young terns. And we did the usual – the
dark box, the snippets of fish force-fed each time this young tern
bit my finger (but as usual, rejected with a no, no, no headshake).
And seeing that one leg was bloody and the other useless I knew
that the best mercy would be to kill this bright young life quickly.
But I was not up to the best mercy. Our tern would have to suf-
fer through our imperfect love, our wish to do better than we are

capable of doing. And in the morning, of course, the tern was still. And that's how it is with luck. Sometimes you outlast nearly every recorded individual of your whole species and make twenty-five round trips from Long Island to Brazil in every kind of weather with no cover whatsoever and you survive a quarter century and raise two-dozen broods of auspicious bright-eyed babes. Sometimes you are perfect as anyone but a storm comes too soon. And you're caught in a bad place young and you get smacked too hard to ever stand up again. It's just luck. It's not you.

HOMELESS

David Gessner

Strange to have come through the whole century and find that the most interesting thing is the birds. Or maybe it's just the human mind is more interesting when focusing on something other than itself.
— JOHN HAY

I remember the weeks after the towers fell being particularly beautiful along the coast. While human beings were convinced that nothing would ever be the same, the natural world carried on as it always had. The edges of the darkening eel grass still glistened silver and the cranberry bog reddened before harvest and the swallows gathered in great congregations, laying claim to people's lawns. Those were the tree swallows, but it was their cousins, the bank swallows, that most interested me. Every day I would take my coffee down to the beach and stare back up at the clay bank where they nested below our house. It might sound quaint and pastoral, but it wasn't, not exactly. It was incongruous really: nature striding along on its usual procession toward winter, while for us, despite all the politicians crying for "normalcy," nothing felt normal.

The birds were a joy to watch, though. Their white, shining, sky-skimming bellies shone as they darted every which way, mimicking the bugs they chased, tearing through the air. They flew crazy eights and then crazy nines, finally boomeranging back to their holes, their muscular superhero bodies standing guard on twigs outside the dark caverns. Even when they finally departed their homes for the winter, I kept checking in each morning, hoping to catch sight of a straggler.

As for our own home, my wife and I were entirely in love with it. It sat up on a small perch, above the bank where the swallows nested, and stared out at whatever show happened to be playing that morning on Cape Cod Bay. I had a small study with a view of the water, and from the house I had seen whales breach and coyotes climb up over the bank. We were renters, but we dreamed of buying a house on Cape Cod, of staying there forever. Being home.

※

What animal doesn't take pleasure in hollowing out, building, re-furnishing, or otherwise improving their homes? No doubt the swallows experience some deep encoded pleasure as they tunnel their way into clay banks. The bluff below the house where we resided was perfect bank swallow habitat. No doubt they had been nesting there for hundreds of generations, in all likelihood beginning not long after the last great ice wall receded. The clay wall of the bluff and its environs provided them with exactly what they were looking for: a bank high enough to keep predators away but easy to dig into, and a body of water nearby to give them open airspace during their flights after insects. Extremely social birds, they would hover and flutter around their nests when not on the hunt for bugs.

Soon after the swallows flew south, I went out to examine the shadowed tunnels that dotted the undercrust of the bluff. The tunnels retreated a couple of feet into the dirt, the birds having lined them with straw and grass. Sometimes, I found small feathers. I knew from my reading that the males dug these holes with their beaks and wings, and, once they were dug out, performed territorial circle flights while singing to attract mates. The females hovered by the holes as they decided which mate, and home, to choose. I also knew that next spring, when the birds returned from the south, they would, after a very short rest, begin a kind of massive spring cleaning, or re-excavation, renovating their old homes.

Watching the swallows in flight was the embodiment of delight, but my reading soon took a darker turn. It is not an unusual turn when reading about animals these days. Construction projects, erosion from sea level and storms, and even well-intended projects to fight erosion and flooding, can alter or destroy the steep banks where swallows nest. "Bank Swallows are aerial insectivores," according to the Cornel Lab website, "a group that as a whole has recently undergone steep, unexplained declines." And: "Their North American numbers have crashed by an estimated 89% since 1970."

※

For nearly sixty years, the great nature writer, John Hay, lived atop a hill just three miles down the road from us in the town of Brewster on Cape Cod. His home, like Thoreau's, was a cabin in the woods surrounded by pitch pines and scrub oak.

I went to see John Hay not long after 9/11, hoping perhaps that he could dispense some wisdom. But he was as frazzled and uprooted as everyone else, and the terrorist attacks seemed to confirm something in him about where the world was heading. He believed that we were in the midst of a massive epidemic of self-induced homelessness and exile.

"People are on the run everywhere these days," he said. "As if they don't know where they live. Everyone seems intent on dispossessing themselves."

"The worst thing we've been doing over the past years is to forget about localities," he continued. "You forget about localities – individual places – and it's much harder to find out where you live. When I first moved here, I knew an old Cape Codder who said this place was getting filled up with people who didn't know where they were. And when you are displaced you start to think everything is money – money is the only purpose for so many people now and they just accept this mindlessly."

I thought of something that another Cape writer, Bob Finch, had said to me about John Hay's early years on Cape Cod: "That first flush of rootedness is unrepeatable."

My wife and I had felt some of this first flush, but we knew ours was a more temporary experience than John's. We had dreamed of living in a place, perhaps the place above the swallows, and watching the years go round, learning the place. But my own experience had not been one of steadfast rootedness. All the movement of my life, all the uncertainty, had started shaking a long-cherished pastoral dream from my head. I could no longer read the sub-genre of literature that celebrated the permanence of true home. I had begun to question the idea of an idyllic pastoral cabin in the woods.

Somehow with our rootless lives, children had never been in the cards, but now we found our minds re-ordering themselves. To our own surprise we were delighted by the prospect.

The miscarriage is too painful to recount, but in its aftermath, inspired by something Nina had read, I built a small shrine of sea glass in a patch of dune up the beach from where the swallows nested. When Nina became pregnant again, and I, turning suddenly responsible after twenty years as a ner-do-well, took a teaching job in Boston and then, when that job ended, a "permanent" position at a university in North Carolina.

Our final spring on Cape Cod would also prove the final spring for the house by the sea. It was sold and torn down to make way for a new, bigger house. I was back visiting on Cape Cod the day they demolished the house. I thought seeing the house go would be the worst moment, but it wasn't. The worst moment came the next morning, when I was walking down the beach and noticed that the bank below the house, the one that had been home to the bank swallows, had been torn up by bulldozers. Rocks were being hauled in to build a seawall where the bank had been. I didn't blame the new owners, who were just looking to shape and protect their own home. But I imagined the swallows returning the following May to look for their homes as they had for hundreds of generations. Imagined them finding their homes not just torn up but entombed in stone.

Later I would draw some conclusions about how we had come to leave Cape Cod. But at the moment of leaving I could say little with certainty. I only knew that we were saying goodbye to the place where we'd thought we were meant to live, and that we were doing so as new parents. And I knew that mine would not be John Hay's story, a story of long rooting. For us there would be no cabin in the woods.

Birder Cats
Bill Hilton Jr.

I love my birds, the woman said,
I feed them all year 'round.
I love my Fluffy cat as well,
I got her at the pound.
I feed the birds with seeds and corn,
I put it on the ground.
And when the cat goes out to play
Sometimes I'm not around.

I know my Fluffy likes my birds
And chases them for fun.
I've never seen her hurt a bird,
None, not even one.
My Fluffy wouldn't kill a bird,
But she might make it run.
Oh, she might swipe at tail or wing,
With that she would be done.

I found a dead bird on my stoop,
The head and leg were gone.
It must have been a hungry owl,
Catching migrants before dawn.
I know it wasn't Fluffy,
She's resting on the lawn.
Fluffy'd never bite a bird,
She'd just lie there and yawn.

I call myself a birder,
And I do love my cat.
Fluffy is a birder, too,
I'm very sure of that.

She watches them intently,
From right there where she's at.
Beside that dead bird's carcass,
Placed on the front porch mat.

PLUMMETING

Rochelle L. Johnson

There is a poetics of grief, just as there is a poetics of migration. Both involve pattern and form. A grieving heart takes on a sort of pattern, just as migrating birds move together in a form. There is a rhythm and resolution to both, too. We presume peace and perhaps even some joy will return to the grief-stricken, and migrating birds trust, in their birdlike way, that they too will find resolution – in blossoms, berries, or barnacles – at flight's end.

But the poetics are failing these last few summers. The patterns and rhythms shatter as temperatures rise and some birds migrate early, only to find their nesting grounds gripped by unusual heat. Hot, dry conditions damage nestlings permanently within their first few days of life. In India, in England, all around the world, scorching temperatures mean heat-exhausted birds literally plummeting from the sky, dead and dying. We have warmed the earth beyond birds' abilities to thrive. And we have created a planet that surpasses our own capacities for grieving.

Last summer, infant Caspian terns sought to escape record Pacific-Northwest heat by leaping from their rooftop nests only to be seared by the asphalt below. Journalists devised new phrases to communicate the tragedy: the *heat dome* had caused a *mortality event*, a *mass bird death* costing some two hundred lives. Only some reporters mentioned that human beings of developed nations have so destabilized the climate that temperatures can exceed the powers of bird biology. This summer is no better: that entire colony has been displaced, nests and unhatched eggs abandoned to the sun, a new generation of terns lost to the region, to the skies, to time.

I know: you are tired of tales of environmental sorrow. Some of my most eco-minded friends say they are *done* with feeling sadness over their part in the planet's losses. It is too much to sort through, too much to bear. But I must dwell here a while, because the loss of those Caspian terns exposes some crucial layers of climate calamity. And there may be a poetics here, too.

Those adult terns chose industrial roofs as nesting sites because nearby piles of ash on asphalt looked like sandy hills on beaches. Birds can no longer identify proper habitat in our manufactured world. Compounding their disorientation, the severe heat causes their body-chemistry to fail, brain-circuits to misfire. Perhaps most disturbing is that most of us resist feeling the sorrow such an event brings. We bury this grief deep down, somewhere below the desiccated carcasses, a depth most of us feel only as numbness.

Perhaps I am especially compelled to this dark remorse because I have been here before. There was a first time when I unthinkingly killed, and then grieved, migratory birds. I was young and foolish, a New Englander visiting a new lover in Louisiana's steamy richness. The morning air was thick with wet when my lover and I paddled his green canoe onto a Spanish moss-draped lake outside of town. Painted turtles plopped from drifting logs, and alligator-eyes blinked heavy alongside bald-cypress knees. The muskrat-like bodies of nutria crisscrossed the canoe's path, their coral-colored teeth chewing grasses, reeds, everything that swayed. Dark-headed cottonmouths parted the duckweed carpeting the water. That whole place was slippery.

We left the tree-studded swamp and paddled into denser thickets. We leaned forward in our seats, reaching our necks toward our knees to duck under crooked boughs. Soon we dropped our paddles in the belly of the canoe and grasped the branches of surrounding buttonbush, pulling the boat deeper into the brambles. Wedged in a tangled grove, we joked that if it weren't for the alligators we could make love here, hidden to all but the tree frogs. Only then did we look up and see: we were making trouble.

We were in the middle of a rookery, the view upward a canopy of birds. In this garden of cypress, we were like terrorists, and the scene exploded into a shrapnel of flailing wings. Startled white ibis took flight, their black-tipped wings alighting in agitation. Dozens of other birds fled in a full palette of color: green and tricolored herons rising alongside the indigo of little blues, the black of grunting cormorants joining the lavender-gray of great blue herons. Crimson-pink roseate spoonbills rocketed. Snowy egrets tore away, their shimmering wispy white splays streaks of lightning shooting skyward.

We quickly sought an exit. Just ahead of us, the long necks of two adult anhingas arced upward from a branch. Their bolting bodies soon became small, dark crosses in the sky, but their three babies remained in the nest. Not six feet from my face, each fragile nestling stirred like the head of a dandelion in an impending storm, pappus shuttering. The chicks raised their twig-thin necks from a tussle of black-and-white feathers fluffed over wheat-colored down. Each tiny beak seemed a mere bristle on a cotton ball – until they opened their mouths, crying for their parents and for their very lives. With one good pull on the bush at my side, I could have reached them, cupped their soft bellies in my palm. But those babies did what evolution leads us to do when trauma becomes too great to bear: one by one, they leapt.

They leapt, but they could not yet fly. They dove, but they could not yet swim. Each nearly weightless ball became a ripple, fading into stillness.

Even then, we tried to fool ourselves. My lover told me that those infants would survive. He said they only needed us to keep moving. They were waiting for us to be gone, and then they would surface and breathe. I said those birds were made to swim anyway. Any second, their parents would return, dive, and rescue their children. But we both knew this was fool's talk, like the assurances new lovers give themselves and each other even as they realize their relationship has little chance of survival.

You now see why, these past summers, plummeting terns recalled for me drowned anhingas from long ago. Both sets of nestlings experienced the nervous system taxed to brokenness. Both were victims of the voracious desire of self-absorbed human beings. Both remind us that to numb ourselves to even the most tragic losses is to continue our dalliance with violence and duplicity. It is to cling to limerence over love.

My path eventually diverged from that Louisiana lover's, our romance now a brief memory in my life – just as humanity's passionate affair with extravagant extraction and conspicuous consumption will occupy a short, fatal episode in the history of human being. But I long felt the weight of those featherlight birds who plummeted to their deaths on that humid morning. In time, I made myself move through that grief. I touched its broken patterns and explored its disrupted rhythms. And then I emerged someone new, vowing to stay with the birds still living, faithful.

I learned to identify the birds by their calls, shapes, and names. I chart their autumn migrations. I memorize their colors and watch as their forms dapple the spring leaves. I listen for winter songs. I want to believe they know my regret in harming their kin, that we recognize each other's fragility. I need to believe they hold hope for humanity just as I yearn for their resilience.

When we are honest with ourselves, we grieve fully not merely the sufferings of birds but our own role in their devastations. For we perform yet another type of violence when we conceal our grief over this waning world. Grief changes people. Grief enables the living to reimagine their lives, releasing death's numbing. Through grief, we renew our meaning. Perhaps we might understand even the darkness of climate grief as having its own migratory poetics, a pattern and form and rhythm that can carry us toward a renewed inhabitation of this world.

Poetics can save lives. Poetics might keep nestlings nestled in nests and migratory birds from drowning in skies of fire.

Blue Heron
Deborah Levoy

Let a blue heron nest in my heart
This is how I start
Let my hands turn currents in rivers
Let me feel the shiver

May she weave my weary bones
Into the leaves that twine her home
May my eyes shine with her dreams
The world is more than it seems

Let a blue heron fledge in my marrow
Let her lead, I will follow
Let my arms bend as she takes wing
This is how I sing

May she fly to peaceful waters
With her regal sons and daughters
May my eyes shine with her dreams
The world is more than it seems

When I batten down against tomorrow
Squeezing so tight to avoid the sorrow
As if I control the ebb and flow
And despite my endless schemes
The universe slips and streams

Let her mighty wings, sweep clean my mind
So that I might find
Words that branch like deepest canyons
With feathered laughter as companions

May they still my fevered fright
So I reflect the deepest night
May my eyes shine with her dreams
The world is more than it seems

How I Spend My New Summers
Renata Golden

I watch pyrocumulous clouds rise from the ridgeline
and shut my windows to save myself from the smoke.
Daily operational updates on Facebook keep me informed
of progress made by the fire and the fire crews but not
of the deer and the elk and the rattlesnakes and
especially not of high elevation birds during nesting season.

Rivers of robins
stream past in late October
Nowhere else to go

Autumn Farewell
Blessing for the Migratory Birds
Tina Asherae Fields

Fall Equinox: the leaves turn gold
And you wise birds heed the call to South.

Farewell, winged beauties.
How we will miss you!
My heart aches upon your leaving.

All I can offer are my blessings:

As you journey, may you find
nourishment at every stop:
plants offering rich seeds,
green beds beckoning through built deserts,
respite from predators,
lift upon thermals,
kindness from thunderclouds,
a place to rest on vast dark water.

May you travel in good company
of kindred flying above and below,
led by stars and the memory maps of ancestors.

And when the seasons have turned; when the time is right,
may you rise together,
bank your bodies on gentle winds,
speed your way into the northerly sky,
and hear our rejoicing when you return,
heralding Spring.

Come Back to Me
Jamie K. Reaser

Why must you go?
I had just become used to you,
to the landscape with you in it.
You were a presence
I was counting on.

Why this change in appearance?
Why this sudden departure?
What of your needs weren't
being met in this place,
this place with me in it?

Come back to me.
Come back to me like a bird
returns in the spring –
famished and full of song.
Come back to me.
Won't you come back to me?

Your voice was my rising.
Your company, my joy.
Did I not offer you enough?
What would have been
worth staying for?
More giftings? More praise?
I would have done more.

Come back to me.
Come back to me like a bird
returns in the spring –
famished and full of song.

Come back to me.
Won't you come back to me?

Come back to me.
Come back to me like a bird
returns in the spring –
famished and full of song.
Come back to me.
Won't you come back to me?

The silence is something terrible!
This homeplace feels so empty.
These short days are long on loneliness.
You left me behind in the winter
of my life.
The cardinal is no consolation.
Crimson is my broken heart.
Sadness is a seed that feeds me.

Come back to me.
Come back to me like a bird
returns in the spring –
famished and full of song.
Come back to me.
Won't you come back to me?

Come back to me.
Come back to me like a bird
returns in the spring –
famished and full of song.

Christmas Party
Derek Sheffield

From cold night air we step through double doors
into bright lights reflecting from a polished floor
and the chatter of sixty-some people.
As my daughter's school friend whisks her away,
her father sees me eyeing the massive beams
spanning the air above his guests. Old-growth,
from Canada, he says, but really I should see
their house in Seattle. He leads me to an array
of catered dishes spread across quartzite countertops.
As I fill my plate, I hear a woman laugh
at the sore losers they are, the people protesting
the president's threats against immigrants.
Behind her, through a wall of glass doors
and shining in the falling snow,
a huge wooden cross strung with white lights.

More talk, wine, more rooms, laughter,
then my daughter, ready to go, and as I reach
for our coats I look down to find a hummingbird
lying on the slats of a heating vent. No
misplaced ornament, I see as I pick it up, but real
iridescence that is less than air on my palm.
My daughter reaches one slim finger toward its wings
stuck in an emerald *x* just as the hostess finds us.
How in the world . . . she exclaims,

and as she does, I see how it slipped through
a door left open at summer's end as they were leaving
for the next house. The door swung shut
and the hummingbird was left to zip and swing
through all that vaulted space, to migrate only

from leather to brass and patter like a great
and solitary bee against sun-splashed windows.
Months later, after such luxury and no way to live,
this shimmery mummy. Another guest walks up,
grabs my wrist, and says, *Oh, can I have it?*
I could make something! reaching for her purse.

Our tires move like whispers through the new snow.
Maybe remembering all the hummingbirds
that blurred their way to our feeders to slip their tongues
into sweet water all summer, my daughter asks
if it will be okay. I stare down the bright tunnel
of our lights, the big flakes falling like so many wings
snipped and sweeping down from above. I can't stop
seeing that woman's black purse, what
in God's name we are making.

TO CELEBRATE

Backyard Migrant Micro Fallout
J. Drew Lanham

Just now; with skies graying and rain threatening a mini-wave of warblers pushed through the three-quarter acre! A dozen butter-butts and a couple of tail-pumping palms found the blooming wild cherry trees to their liking. I heard the sudden intrusion of different songs among the constant calling of cardinals and Carolina wrens. Even the persistent mockingbird's round the clock work didn't dampen the soft trills and calls that foretold the little flock's presence. I watched them picking and pecking; then catching and hammering the little caterpillars they found hiding in the tender new greenery. To an inchworm the little passerine predators may as well have been Harpy eagles.

It is all a matter of perspective, I suppose.

More and more I sit in the fragment of world that the mortgage says is almost mine and wonder on the wanderers I happen to see. It is that rarest of times when expectation often exceeds expectation. That weather or wind – or simple chance – happens to bring them into my tiny sphere is miracle for marveling. The feathered things come whether I wish or not. I count blessings in birds these days. What comes my way next. Time, I suppose, will tell.

Pajaros Migratorios

Américo Yábar (English Translation, Pia Christina Ossorio)

Viajando como pájaro,
migratorio.
Errática, alma mía.
Estas en el mito de
las aves.
Estas en el viento.

Traveling like a bird,
migratory.
Erratic, my soul.
You are in the myth of
birds.
You are in the wind.

Pájaros en horizontes
de viajes largos
parecen pintados
por truenos, vientos
lluvia…
Quien sabe
alegrías, cantos y nostalgias.

Birds on horizons
of long journeys
look painted
by thunder, winds
rain…
Who knows
joys, songs, and nostalgia.

Pájaros erráticos, migratorios
abiertos a toda aventura,
las alas vivas volando
sobre jardines de bellas
flores,
sobre bosques de arboles.
Quien sabe de pensamientos?

Erratic birds, migratory
open to any adventure,
living wings flying
over gardens of beautiful
flowers,
over forests of trees.
Who knows of thoughts?

2

Pájaros migratorios
viajando, viajando,
creando nueva vida.
Llevando semillas
por el mundo.
Circulando, alegría
de vivir en el canto.

Migratory birds
traveling, traveling,
creating new life.
Carrying seeds
around the world.
Circulating, joy
of living in song.

Pájaros migratorios
volando dentro de mi
alma,
saludando al mundo.
Sus desiertos, bosques
y montañas,
saludando sus océanos.
El aura, de la Madre
Cósmica.

Migratory birds
flying in my
soul,
greeting the world.
Her deserts, forests
and mountains,
Greeting her oceans.
The aura of the Cosmic
Mother.

3

Como pájaros migratorios.
Me he sentado a
cantar:
¨Cuando la luna esta
Redonda"
y derrama lágrimas de despedida...

Like migratory birds.
I sat to
sing:
"When the moon is
Round"
and sheds tears of farewell…

Como pájaro luminoso,
Veo el parpadeo estelar.
Cuando la soledad
del viento
y cuando puedo cantar
en una rama de mi ser interno,
canto para aliviar el dolor de alguien.
Canto al amanecer.
Canto al atardecer.
Oigo el silencio del viento.

Like a luminous bird,
I see the stars flicker.
When the solitude
of the wind.
and I can sing
on a branch of my internal self,
I sing to ease someone's pain.
I sing at dawn.
I sing at sunset.
I hear the silence of the wind.

Nighthawks in Migration
Steve A. Patterson, Jr.

I know the place to wait for them,
a field whose weeds grow well,
healthy with grass, sparse of trees.
Between the earth and rising moon
insects fly, mocking all who can't.

Other mocking, too, needs nothing
as elegant as sky in which to
curdle hope. Whether from
malevolent source or lack of care
my human kind do wear the name:

unjust, diseased, violent, selfish fools.
Grace is there to free us back to life,
yet disbelieved by those who worship
only what they prove. What can inspire
and reignite to purge this tragic fate?

They are coming, like Jesus is coming,
but sooner, and more often, riding
feathered blades, brown trumpets
of gospel mud for eyes
who lost original will to see.

Bird Watching
Curt Meine

Amid atrocities and injustices, unwatchable news,
refugee tales and unspeakable cruelties,
after such losses, and knowing the ground
quakes with bitterness and unleashed angers,
energies wasted in a time of need to no good end,
and heaviness pulls even the most buoyant down,
from on high up above it just seems so obvious:
it's the birds who watch us, and watch over us,
keep us untethered and able to connect,
stitch and bind the world whole, migrating
their lines to trace the lifeways of all together.
Odd to the see a crane headed that way.
That's the female calling, searching for a mate.
That kestrel could hardly hold on to that mullein top.
That high-pitched waxwing, see her perched there?
Yet let us also give praise to the first trill chorus frog,
and gratitude for friends, walking sticks, and ancients.

Moment of Beyond
Steve A. Patterson, Jr.

Red
crossbills
pry open cones
of mountain hemlock trees.

Noisy
exposure
so high above
the cold granite peak.

Sudden
departure,
fling back across
the gray disbelieving sky.

Speak for the Birds
Donna & Kelly Mulhollan

Abstract artist Morris Graves,
his images of birds are etched on my brain.
I remember when Kurt Vonnegut said,
"I wish we'd all been born birds instead"
I adore Audubon's Snowy Owl,
his wonderful drawings of waterfowl.
I love Mary Oliver's Catbird poem
It speaks to my heart and lifts my soul.
Musicians, artists & lovers of words,
let's paint & sing and SPEAK FOR THE BIRDS!

Grasshopper sparrow, meadowlark
Saw-whet owl praying in the dark
American robin, Franklin's gull
It's hard to watch your numbers fall
California condor, little field sparrow
The road is long and the path is narrow
Blackbird singing in the dead of night
Over to the sweet by and by

Dr. Seuss was a hero to me,
he made the Lorax speak for the trees.
Birds need advocates of their own
a painted prayer, song, or poem.
Maya Angelou's words sprouted wings
when she wrote about how a caged bird sings.
Thanks you photographers, great big thanks,
I love your photos of the dancing cranes!
Remember Prince, when he was alive
sang about how it sounds, when the Doves Cry.

Chuckwill's widow silently mourning
Boat-tailed grackle cries out a warning
Says his cousin the bobolink and Florida scrub Jay
Loggerhead shrike are fading away
Yellow-billed cuckoo foretelling of rain
Bobwhite quail's forgotten his name
Old ivory bill's no longer heard
Little house wren ain't said a word

Abracadabra...is it black magic?
Where are the birds? Seems they've vanished.
Thrasher, he ain't hanging round,
Wood thrush he ain't made a sound.
When Rachel Carson wrote *Silent Spring*,
she got the whole world trembling.
So many birds are down on their luck,
The pintail and the ring-neck duck.
Musicians, artists & lovers of words
Let's paint & sing and SPEAK FOR THE BIRDS
Let's paint & sing and SPEAK FOR THE BIRDS

Thrushing
Pamela Norton Reed

So I'm following this thrush
[Except it may be a robin
because I don't quite know any better,
   though the alleged robin likely does]

Above, a definite robin
   sweetly, drunkenly, entices me.

Thirty yards ahead,
   my thrush is leading me on
hopping forward,
      deeper into the forest
      pausing to
      peek
back
         to see
Am I following him?

Yes.   I'm following him.

He seems pleased
   and hops onward
Eeee oh lay

The light hits my bird
   streaming in through a sudden break in the pines
      And yes. He is,
      all
      wood
      thrush.

He flies to a low bough to trill
Eeee oh *lay*
   His voice a flute
      calling me.

Off any known trail,
   I trail,
         entranced.
   That hop in his walk
      – the sweet thrill of his song –
   Feeling our way forward,
      I'm on the verge of Thrushing
               as I shadow him in shadows

And I wonder
   Is he wooing me?
Because I can be wooed.
   If I follow
      Will he chase me in silent circle?
Beg me to rest beside him
      then leave perch to romance me again?
Will my thrush beguile me?
      enchant me to stay?
            to nest?

Ee ohh Lay

   I choose you, my thrush
   We will be we
for at least this morning.

So I'm following
         this
   wood
            thrush

A Hinge Has Opened on Hard Times but the First Sparrow Sings Again
John Lane

And the song
pours down
the walls.
The warmth
rises. The sky
is so blue. Notes
pool in deep
gulleys, reserved
dark. I am happy
it turned out
this way, at least
one more day.

I'táámaʼpiiwa
Cristina Eisenberg

Guided by instinct
    zugunruhe
       and a prayer
           strength
      discipline

    Propelled by winds
      of change
          wings of hope
             dreams
                  I soar
          past
        siloed souls
      barren wheat fields
    burnt woods

               Following the light
                 toward wonder
                       liberation
                the far horizon
          all my relations

           Where the
    Wise Ones help
            the Seventh Generation
                     find reciprocity
               justice
           heal survive
         thrive
     love
   live
be

I'tááma'piiwa
it's a beautiful dawn
A'ho

The Yellow Warbler
Jamie K. Reaser

Bold and bright,
with a soul-stirring desire
to couple and nest and tend
he sings from the willow branch,
and the day
is suddenly delightful
to every living thing –
the awakened and arrived.
Spring!
The cold wintered-heart
cracks, melts, reveals
a reason to keep on living,
and doing so with blessings
counted out in the open, unabashedly.
You've noticed, right?
in your very own chest,
and you've listened, yes?
and you've called out, haven't you?
for the company
that could turn a solitary moment
into a renewal of faith
in the worth of tomorrow,
and perhaps even the years that follow that.
How could you not?
Oh, whistle sweetly into the blue morning
yellow warbler,
whistle sweetly dear little bird,
dare,
remind us, life is beauteous –
so worth showing up for
with great self-expression

from a high leafy pulpit,
though we may be so deeply tired,
aren't we?
from our long, arduous
journey.

Let there be no excuses.

Purifying the Spirits
April Tierney

Have you ever spoken with someone who lives in a college town? Have you ever listened as they describe the way the town swells in the fall when the students return? How sometimes they are disgruntled by the increased traffic, the longer lines at the bank. But mostly, how their voices ring with wonder as they relate the fervor of so much vibrancy curling around every corner; the stories that all those students carry from the places they spent their summers, the newness blowing in like fresh air to purify the spirits of all who love that town and live there year-round.

This is how it is in my backcountry community each spring when the birds return from their long journeys south. We are never quite sure how much we missed them until we begin to hear their songs rippling through the trees in the warming early mornings, how perceptibly sparse it was for so many months without them.

We were not lonely, per se, as there are other birds who come from the Great White North to take up residence in our hills for the winter. But even still, it is that springtime fervor, with all those stories the returning ones carry from distant lands – the newness blowing in like fresh air to purify our sedentary spirits – that re-enliven this place we collectively claim as home. Their names swell in our throats like the sweetest kind of nourishment and we call them out when we see them, welcoming them back, welcoming them home.

Mountain bluebird. Black-headed grosbeak. Blue grosbeak. Broad-tailed hummingbird. Bullock's oriole. Western tanager. Western wood-pewee. Violet-green swallow. Chipping sparrow. Cordilleran flycatcher. Yellow warbler. Warbling vireo. Plumbeous vireo. Mourning dove. House wren. Lazuli bunting.

Of course there are more, there are always more. Of course these beautiful creatures bear a thousand other names. Of course these are the names we have given them as settlers, and their bodies remember the names that were sung into the breeze by the Indigenous Peoples of these lands – the Cheyenne, Ute, and Arapaho, the Tsis tsis'tas, Nuche, and Hinono'ei – in languages made from the trees, the roots of the trees, the stars, even the moss, and the wind, yes always the wind. Collectively, in all the names that you bear, we welcome you back magnificent birds with multiple homes. Welcome home.

IBÚ KOLÉ

Langston Kahn

A vulture-headed woman in a yellow dress wants me to follow her
into the sky, but I cannot. Sticky black vines hold me back. I try to
rip them off, but they are inside me too – and if I pull too hard my
chest will crack open. I wake up on a mat on the floor, sweating.
    That was the morning of my initiation.

When I was a boy, I would fly in my sleep. If I focused just right,
I could lift off and soar, gliding through the dream time – an
experience so visceral, I would wonder as I woke if I had actually
learned a new life skill.
    As a Queer Black boy uprooted from Washington Heights
and deposited in Real-Housewives-White-New Jersey, I learned
to migrate to fantasy worlds to protect my heart.

Books were my wings of choice to these worlds. I always had a pile of two-to-three on hand in case of emergency. But, that kind of constant travel is hard on the body.

Buried pain without presence to metabolize it turns malignant. Denied emotions become disease to call you back home. I learned to swallow micro-aggressions and manage the emotions of others as a survival strategy. I was in and out of the hospital with stomach issues, unable to digest my life. The more my body suffered, the less I felt any desire to stay on Earth.

※

But now, I go to the river. Clothes cut away. I make myself a sacrament to Oshun – River Goddess – deity of my ancestors – and she kills me so I can live. I watch what flows away, soon to be an offering to the flighted scavengers.

One of the oldest aspects of Oshun is Ibú Kolé – She Who Collects and Recovers the Garbage and Dust. The Vulture-Headed One. She is the Golden Lady. Essence of Joy.

The fearful blame vultures for bringing Death – see them as ill omens. But if you spend time with the Turkey Vulture People, it is hard not to love them. Their scientific name, *Cathartes aura*, may be translated as Golden Purifier. They are intelligent, sweet, and playful. They will get attached to people and follow them around like a puppy or a watchful grandmother, if you let them.

Vultures play tag as they wheel through the air, gliding, wings unflapping, keen olfactory sense guiding them towards decaying flesh. With their naked red crowns, they enter into the rot and disease of carcasses and transmute refuse into nourishment. Their stomach biome neutralizes bacteria and viruses. They do not need to kill to nourish themselves. They simply process what gets left behind, leaving ecosystems healthier in their wake. They can stomach what others cannot.

Vultures too are beings that cross between worlds. Up and

down. Sky and earth. They migrate south to warmer climes when it is cold, navigating by the Earth's magnetism. A few months later, they return.

My people did not migrate, they were stolen. Shackled. Brought to a strange land full of strange people. Beaten if they spoke their languages, sang their songs. Mother torn from son, torn from brother, torn from sister. The names of their dead erased. Forced to hide their relationship with the holy powers – Oshun and so much more. Forced as chattel to build the wealth of a stillborn culture already decaying.

Yet, even in strange land, they could feel that magnetic pull back home. And, so they sprouted wings. They were not freed, but created their freedom. They digested the rotting culture they were fed. They metabolized it, weaving new languages, songs, dances, foods – nourishing all creation.

※

Leaving the forest I am reborn.
Clad in white cloth, with red on my crown.
Holding a jar of river water.

I still migrate to other worlds, but I do not leave my body behind. Just as Vultures honor the Earth's rhythms and directions from their elders, moving seasonally towards abundance, I am learning to let pleasure guide me as I co-create with the unseen world and remember myself whole.

I no longer swallow bitterness and indulge in addictive escape. I am apprenticed to Vulture – transmuting pain with compassion and presence.

I am carefully, tenderly, ministering to the dead. My ancestors are clear with me. "Grandchild do not think our resilience, creativity, and love came from surviving that mess. Those gifts got us through the horrors but slavery itself was just a waste of time. Do not allow your heart to be bound by what we sacrificed to free you from." I listen. Carrying forward their gifts and laying the bones to rest.

I am picking through the refuse of culture, discerning what can be good nourishment and what must be returned to the Earth so She can make something new. For the safety of our young, and in service of those who are coming, I clean up what I can.

Vultures clear the way for the living. Vultures clear the way for Life to flow. I am learning to follow the scent of Death as a call towards Life. I am learning there is no place Joy is absent from when we choose to center Her.

My wings are outstretched.
I am flying home.

Hummingbird
Pamela Uschuk

Slashed into the rufous chest
a throat like a chunk of neon ruby
gives him away as he whirs
to his mate perched in blackberry bramble
spread beneath our windows.
Thief of sunlight,
spangled,
pure infrared,
hummingbird shakes kinetic wings
and he is off.
No sloth, he revs
to fifth gear,
torqued so high, he
does not fly so much
as bee buzz
straight lines stunning air
or diving to stab at us
who wander too close
to his intended nest.
We whose imaginations only reach

such velocity confronting
possibilities
like love or lust or death,
must watch, amazed
at lightning's bloody jewel.
Hummingbird, tongue-sized,
bright articulator of spirits,
you attack all intruders,
hawks and wrens alike.
Even from shadows

you manufacture light.
Teach us your courage these days
when fire takes the world,
your tenderness
as you take rare rest,
yawn, then shiver
in your perfect wings
daring such gravity as finally grounds us.

An Unexpected Joy
Jeanine M. Canty

I hear magic whiz by
An unexpected joy
No need to look and try to catch this
You are here

The precious cycle has gone round again
The cold, gray contemplations bring new green ones
Swirled with pinks, reds, and allochromatic possibilities
Fresh start, new skin, open windows

Broad-tailed hummingbird, both usher and initiator of summer
A deep whirling blur of beauty, endless movement
Weightless, fast, dazzling

It is said that the hummingbird symbolizes joy
Of whose joy is unclear
The joy must belong to the beholder of such vibrancy and speed
A cacophony of metal crickets, zinging with declaration

All accolades center on the male broad-tailed hummingbird
The female masked within more subtle hues and sound
Relegated to later migration, tending of the nest and brood,
    lacking stardom

Is this the pattern?
Binary gender roles
The layout quickly ruffles feathers
Injustice at the rigidity, sadness on translation
Would nature bind us so formally?
Never to shine, always to serve

An emergent property!
The female Jacobin hummingbird has mastered biological
   ornamentation
She has multiplied her powers with the ability to appear as the
   male
Her hunting grounds expanded; her colors brightened
They speculate the other female species may do the same

Magnificent vibrancy for utilitarian purpose
Nonduality as freedom and aspiration
Skillful means, using radiance to serve
And cloaking once again within simplicity

The cool air rushes in, billowing the first leaves of autumn
Creation's kaleidoscope fading; the party goers slowly depart
Goodbye summer, you are so appreciated
Treasures immeasurable, the brightness of life

Time to close the windows and turn to the descent
Her young brood has flown off in independence
Her mate has left again
Time to find home once more
You are here
An unexpected joy

Dawn Chorus
Kathleen Dean Moore

Who among us has not seen the image of the Earth from space, as the planet turns under the light of the sun, and morning advances? Always half spangled black, half glistening blue and green, the ball rolls, and mountains and coastlines, seas and continents slowly emerge into the sun. It stirs me, I have to say, to watch satellite video of morning flowing over the Earth like a bright tide. I imagine boats full of brass choirs, bumping along the advancing edge of the flow, heralding the morning.

But in fact, that's almost exactly what has happened every day for, how many days? Sixty million years, so 21,900,000,000 days. For that many days, there have been birds that stir in the breeze that precedes the sunrise, lift their heads, and begin to sing. The "dawn chorus," people call it, the especially brilliant bird songs that begin the day.

Who knows why birds pour out their hearts first thing in the morning? Maybe the air is cool and sound travels farther. Maybe the morning, before the foraging gets good, is spare time that the birds fill with singing, the avian analogue of a second cup of coffee. Probably singing in the morning demonstrates fitness, saying, "I am strong, I am fully alive, I have lived through the night and emerged full-throated from my dark shelter with energy and joy to spare." All good reasons to sing.

Recording artists have followed the sun around the world, recording the dawn chorus on continent after continent, the great unrolling of song as the Earth turns: again, that tide of sparkling light advancing over the darkness, lifting song after song. Imagine the magic of this planet. Dear god, we live on a music box that plinks out music as the Earth turns. No, we live on something even more magical than a music box, because pink morning light, not little metal pins, plucks the prongs. Who could have the whimsy and aesthetic abandon to invent such a marvelous machine? Who would not treasure it and pass it down, carefully preserved, to the children?

August Is
Coreen Weilminster

August is a threshold.
On one side – summer
The other – autumn

In that liminal space a transition zone
Where sky is an unnamed hue of blue
Sunlight, a mellow embrace – warm and golden and ripe.
Winged things find their magic here.

August is a shapeshifter.
Within the shift a restless energy
Of monarch,
Yellowjacket
And swallow,
Of hummingbird
And hawk.

But also a settling,
A comfort
Of bloom
And fledge
And forage
Complete.

August is the caul of each year.
Between the veil
A bittersweet symphony:
Cicada seismic swagger
Gives way
To cricket trill.
Song sparrow relinquishes its crisp morning herald
To jagged alarm of blue jay and crow.

August is a masterpiece.
A canvas where the landscape softens and
Grasses soothe the serious line of horizon
Through a brushstroke of plume,
A gentle sweep of gold,
Impressionistic perfection in sunlight gone to seed.
Winged migrants change too
Sporting a different ensemble for their southward return

August is a zeitgeist.
It is time and space
Where ripe brown oak gall eclipses
Tiny green acorn on same branch
And milkweed leaf holds egg, larva, pupa, and adult all at once.
It is a spirit trapped "in between"
Whose lowing is the sound
Of wind
And thermal
And starlight
Calling the restless home.

Mandorla (Fall Crossing)
Kim Schnuelle

HEADING SOUTH

There is no hurry
turning wing to flight.
A frost at dawn is reason enough,
or perhaps a flaming columbine
wilted now in broken grass
He swings upward,
circling once over cold waters,
breath fast under scarlet feathers.
He will not hide
in a swallow's murmuration,
but migrates unattended.
Four thousand miles in crossing
down past deserts below.

The landmarks remain.
A windless marsh by the Exxon station,
syrup feeders on café patios
fresh tended at dawn,
the fields of paintbrush and penstemons
by the freeway off ramp.
Familiar, he knows the route.
Another sunrise and he will be
halfway there.

HEADING NORTH

Hurry Hurry, *mija*. *Ten prisa*.
Hear that pop, that scream,
just over the hill?
There is no time.
Grab your red shoes,
click your heels three times.
Take us north,
far from this place.

It's cold in the boxcar
that rumbles dolefully past
idle ranches, dusty bougainvillea.
We are alone, yes,
but *duermate ahora, chica*
not all birds move in flocks.
Palenque, Veracruz, Zacatecas
will pass in the night.
They are mere ghosts,
specters to ignore.
Rest now. Rest until the
crossing.

Here is where we exit;
Here is where it starts.
There is no *río*, no *estanque*,
no road to guide us.

He remembers the shallow pond,
the mesquite and acacia,
the place of water and rest.
But the man, the child,
lain flat by arroyo banks,
they are new.

Perched high on ocotillo bloom
vermillion spark grabs the sky.
He watches them fall
face down in the tepid *charco*.
They drink deeply then dream,
sleeping benumbed and silent,
but safe now,
as he lifts skyward,
turning towards Mexico.

But the fence is broken
two miles east.
Another sunrise,
to *el otro lado.*

It is not yet midday,
yet I can't leave the shade.
I feel the blood,
crimson, pulsing under your
neck.
We must seek the birds now,
they are our hope.
Look there, *mija!*
A rufous hummingbird,
all the way from Canada he is!
Finally, our good luck.
He will find water.

And only in this time, this crossing
are we as one.
Heart and wing at rhythm,
this place, this mandorla,
I will remember forever.

Namu Namu Chirp Chirp[1]

Frank Inzan Owen

> *Bend your ear to the songs of the birds,*
> *and they will be singing the universal truth.*
> — FROM THE *JEN T'IEN YEN MU* BY CHIH CHAO-CHUAN

[Narrator Reads:]
Here in the slow light of morning
let us bend our ears
to the wisdom being sung!

**[Performers or Assembled Participants Recite with
Enthusiasm:]**
namu[2] *namu chirp chirp!*
namu namu chirp chirp!

[Narrator Reads:]
It's on the wind!
It's in the branches!
It's on rooftops
treetops
on roadside fences!

---

1 a call-and-response for ages 5-9, and the ever-young

2 *namu* is a Japanese Buddhist term of praise which translates loosely as
"in the name of…" For purposes of this call-and-response poem, par-
ticipants can insert their own praise-word or phrase (e.g. "all hail") or
culturally appropriate terms for "name" e.g. Afrikaans: *naam*, Bengali:
naam, Catalan: *nom*, Chinese: *namo*, Danish: *navn*, Dutch: *naam*,
Finnish: *nimi*, French: *nom*, German: *name*, Greek: *ónoma*, Hebrew:
shem, Hindi: *naam, nama*, Icelandic: *nafn*, Irish: *ainm*, Italian: *nome*,
Portuguese: *nome*, Spanish: *nombre*, Ukrainian: *nazva*, Uzbek: *nomi*,
Yiddish: *nomen*, Zulu: *igama*, or Esperanto: *nomo*

[Performers or Assembled Participants Recite with Enthusiasm:]
namu namu chirp chirp!
namu namu chirp chirp!

[Narrator Reads:]
The SEASON is changing!
The season is CHANGING!
The season IS changing!

[Performers or Assembled Participants Recite with Enthusiasm:]
THE SEASON IS CHANGING!
THE SEASON IS CHANGING!
namu namu chirp chirp!
namu namu chirp chirp!

[Narrator Reads:]
Days are getting shorter!
Nights are getting *l - o - n - g - e - r*!
Cooler days are blowing in!

[Performers or Assembled Participants Recite with Enthusiasm:]
COOLER DAYS ARE BLOWING IN!
COOLER DAYS ARE BLOWING IN!
namu namu chirp chirp!
namu namu chirp chirp!

[Narrator Reads:]
The Feathered Tribes are gathering!
The longing to travel is spinning within them!
Soon they will take flight!

[Performers or Assembled Participants Recite with Enthusiasm:]
SOON THEY WILL TAKE FLIGHT!
SOON THEY WILL TAKE FLIGHT!
namu namu chirp chirp!
namu namu chirp chirp!

[Narrator Reads:]
Shimmering and colorful!
Luminous rainbow-bright!
Dusky, brown, gray, and light!
The Feathered Tribes are leaving!

[Performers or Assembled Participants Recite with Enthusiasm:]
THE FEATHERED TRIBES ARE LEAVING!
THE FEATHERED TRIBES ARE LEAVING!
namu namu chirp chirp!
namu namu chirp chirp!

[Narrator Reads, Demonstrating a Wave and a Bow:]
Send them off with a wave and bow
until they return with Springtime's blooming!

[ALL:]
WE'LL WELCOME YOU BACK WITH THE WARMTH AND THE LIGHT!
WE'LL WELCOME YOU BACK WITH THE WARMTH AND THE LIGHT!
namu namu chirp chirp!
namu namu chirp chirp!

The Calling
Bob Ford

He teaches me, again, how to build a fire. How to lay in kindling and logs not too tight: the flow of air converts spark to flame—even for our backyard fire. Our seldom used fire ring resides away from the white wooden garage, near the clothesline, over towards the apple tree. We can get away with that—a backyard fire—here on the rural edge of a Memphis suburb. The Mississippi River is a short drive but a long bike ride away. Stars reveal themselves as the fire finds it has a life of its own.

We sit. We wait. We talk in hushed tones so that we can listen for them.

"What do you want for Christmas?"
"Patch up your bike tire, yet?"

We wait. We share leftover Thanksgiving turkey on white bread, and a hot chocolate.

We wait. He hears them first, acknowledged only by a slight nod. Now I hear them. Music. Small talk. Laughter.

It's the geese. I imagine the day at the start of migration, when these geese left James Bay. Did they know they were not to return until next spring? On their way, long V-shapes across the skies over cornfields of the Mid-west. Then, a migration rest stop at the new dawn on a sandbar in the river below Vicksburg. Tonight, I don't know if I can see them here, above the flames. Maybe a shadow or maybe imagination. No matter—it's the conversation I yearn for. It grows louder overhead, more urgent. Plain talk now. They see me, they see the river, forever weaving us all together into the journey. The conversation moves downstream, until I am no longer a part. But now I know. Of rivers and birds, they speak to me of wildness. Of wild things. Of adventure. Of joy. I find this to be Good. My eyes return me to being Earth-bound. I glance across the blaze. My Dad grins.

Haiku: Sandhill Crane Migration Stopover
Tina Asherae Fields

Ancient voices call
From the highest sky, see them?
Sandhill cranes are back!

Flocks of wanderers
Riding the sky on great wings,
Dancing joy at night.

They're too vast to stay,
But one week of their presence
Makes our lives magic.

FEATHERED METRONOMES

Dorinda G. Dallmeyer

I love time. There was the clock which sat on the mantel in my childhood home ticking off the seconds, sounding the hours not with a gentle chime but with a hammer clanging against a steel coil. There were the pocket-watches of the railroad men in the family, who would hold those precision machines up to my ear so I could listen to the rhythm that kept the railroad running.

My first watch had Cinderella pictured on its dial, a daily reminder of what happens when you don't pay attention to time. After that came a watch to celebrate my 16th birthday; my own pocket-watch at graduation, and the waterproof diver's watches that kept me safe on the seabed.

But I also reside among living watches. In my house in the woods where I've lived for 45 years, I watch the hardwoods grow. I can't see through the bark but I know they've put on summer rings and winter rings every year, just the same as time is written in my body.

And faithfully, the birds abide with me in this place, marking time like feathered metronomes. In 45 years of watching the seasons turn, I've encountered 144 species of birds here. Many are the year-round residents long known since childhood. Others pass through in the spring and fall to mark the Earth's place in its orbit. Spring is spangled with the red, black, gold, and yellow of the redstarts flitting like butterflies at the birdbath. In fall, the rose-breasted grosbeaks sit dignified in the feeder, the female traveling in brown tweed, the male dressed in black and white, sporting his raspberry ascot.

Some birds are one-time encounters: a lone blue goose in a winter stubble-field, a bald eagle flying overhead in salute on my birthday. The first Thanksgiving after we moved here, I was on my knees in the front yard setting out plants. I heard a "crawk" above me. Thinking it was a nosy crow, I looked up to see not a crow, but a small flight of sandhill cranes overhead. I dropped my trowel and ran after them as long as I could, but my legs were no match for their strong wings. I watched them disappear over the trees and stood there until their bugling faded as they headed southeast – I hoped, to winter in the Okefenokee.

And then there are the summer residents who come to us from the tropics, so many I have to winnow it down to just a few. The ruby-throated hummingbirds with their flash and stunt-flying are favorites. My husband, David, dutifully serves as their barkeep all summer long, keeping the feeders filled with their favorite beverage.

Others are heard more than seen, with their calls as distinct as the clangor of that old mantel clock. An early arrival is the Louisiana water thrush (a Goliath among my warblers) with its "Chee chi-wit-it chit swee-yuu!" ringing from the creek behind my house. Usually they are hard to observe but I've watched one bobbing and weaving up the creek-bed chasing a crane fly. Others cast about like birddogs on the roof of my house, snapping up fallen caterpillars.

A raucous summer visitor is the great-crested flycatcher with its "Shreep! Shreep!" Whether using our spec-built birdhouses or in a convenient hole in a tree, the birds delight me every time I see, dangling from the entrance, an old snakeskin as part of their home decor.

A bird call familiar from my childhood is the yellow-billed cuckoo, or as I learned it, the "rain crow." Its "Kon, kon, kon" percussive call starts out in rapid staccato repeats, then gradually slows as if it was running out of steam. Folk wisdom has the bird's call as a harbinger of rain, but during a summer's drought, the rain crow sounds way too optimistic.

This bird turns the command "better to be seen and not heard" upside down. It's hard to believe that a bird the size of a blue jay could be that difficult to see in the canopy. But it's stealthy and perfectly counter-shaded. Looking on it from above, it's the same brown as old fallen leaves. From below, its creamy white breast is hard to distinguish against the light from the sun, and its long, dark tail feathers are spotted with white half-moons to break up its silhouette. I've seen them a few times, especially when I'm kayaking and the birds break cover to fly in their signature dipping flight pattern from the trees on one side of the river to the other.

And then, sometimes, they magically appear in full view. I was sitting on the back porch and heard a few whistles from brown-headed cowbirds up in the oaks. The next thing I knew, hundreds of cowbirds were cascading out of the trees to drink at the birdbath there. Cowbirds were everywhere, shoulder to shoulder on the birdbath rim, jostling and standing as tall as possible to intimidate the other birds competing for space and water. The cascades down and flight take-offs up continued like bands of angels descending and ascending Jacob's ladder. And there, on a limb sat a rain crow, calmly hunkered down in its customary pose, watching, and looking satisfied as if to say, "I told you there was water here."

But hardly any bird is anticipated more than the wood thrush. Its fluting "Ee-o-lay, Ee-o-lay, Eee" rings though the woods upon its arrival. And we can almost set our clock by it. Over time, we noticed that they seemed to begin calling right around tax time, and indeed, the records I've kept for the last 22 years show April

13th as the average date of hearing the first "Eee-o-lay." Far beyond the significance of this date on the human calendar is for us to experience their dawn and dusk concerts echoing from the thickets lining the creek, laying down a musical score to announce the start of high spring.

As fall approaches, we begin to lose these players in the soundscape as they begin their southward flights to wintering grounds in the tropics. In their place, white-throated sparrows, kinglets, and maybe some pine siskins will bring their own music along to buoy our spirits during the winter. Time will pass and the Earth will roll on until it's time for the next movement in the concert to start.

Migration Dance
Pepper Trail

We are waiting for the music, hushed and expectant.
Outside the plain church windows, leaves flare
October orange-red. A thrush is perched among them,
flirting its wings, plucking a dark blue berry.
Without hearing, I seem to hear its quiet call.

Within, the concert begins, the sounds of another age,
the harpsichord a jangling handful of keys to locks
forged centuries ago, but still holding the promise
of doors swinging open, of rooms alive with candles
and the brittle grace of antique dancers.

The windows slowly darken and light rain
begins to fall, streaking the glass, bouncing
the bright leaves. The thrush shifts
restlessly, shaking raindrops
from soft impervious feathers.

The violin seems bewitched, driven onward
by Bach's inexhaustible inventions, the player
helpless to resist the elaborations of the musical line,
possessed but also exalted, a lifetime's devotion
fulfilled in the service of irresistible perfection.

Tonight, the thrush will rise to join its fellows,
all flying south through the dark, their bodies dancing
on the lines of magnetic force encompassing the world,
possessed but also exalted, their wings attuned
to timeless music of irresistible perfection.

The concert over, I walk through the leaf-splashed
streets. The rain has passed, and stars appear
through ragged holes of cloud. I imagine
the night sky moving with birds,
and to their music I lift my feet, and dance.

Migrating Fall Birds
Chip Blake

At the car repair place there was a big picture window between the waiting room and the garage, at which you could stand and watch the guys who were working on the cars. When I looked through the window, here's what I saw: six mechanics standing in a circle around my car, some with their arms crossed, some with their hands on their hips, some rubbing their chins and scowling.

I figured that was not good news. And it wasn't, because one of the mechanics eventually came and found me in the waiting room and scrupulously explained that the exhaust system of the car was completely destroyed. Destroyed, furthermore, in a way that no one who worked at the shop had ever seen before. "Front to back, man," he said, "that's what's gotta be replaced." He added that the mechanics were curious to know what I had done to create such damage to the car.

So I had to explain it. In my explanation to him, here's what I left out: that I had been on a birding trip in search of migrating birds, because fall migration has always been my favorite time of the birding year, and that on that day I felt I had to sidestep the day's real-life demands and get out and see what I could find. A majority of birders prefer spring migration, when the birds are dressed in their finery, rushing north to claim the best mates and the best territories, a tinge of desperation in the air. But fall migration, with the birds returning home in a leisurely manner, looking a little replete and self-satisfied and sublime with their efforts of the breeding season, and their faded or molting feathers that can make identification challenging – as a birder, that's my time.

I left that out of my explanation to the mechanic. I also left out that, on my birding expedition that day, I had seen very few birds. It had been a strangely, unsettlingly silent morning, one of the most birdless days I could recall. I sent a text to a birding friend that morning that said "I think all the birds are dead." That was a joke.

But one of the costs of caring about birds is that birdwatchers are always braced for the prospect that the birds will, in fact, diminish, decline, disappear. "Oh, this is the year," you hear yourself thinking, "when I can really tell there are fewer." If you ask any birder about this, you're likely to hear these kinds of concerns corroborated. Every birder worries about it.

I left all that stuff out of the explanation. Here's what I did tell the mechanic: that I had been driving on a poor road in a remote section of a state forest, and that the road became so degraded and rocky that I decided not to continue. There was no place to turn around on this narrow old road, so I had gone in reverse for a long, long way. At some point, while backing up, there was a giant crunch that sent a huge shudder through the frame of the car and made me wince.

I got the car turned around. But it was clear right away that something was wrong – the car sounded like one of those motorcycles that has been fitted with an aftermarket muffler that makes it sound like an F-16. It was deafening. I drove out of the state forest and right to the nearest mechanic I could find.

The mechanic conjectured on what had happened: that I had hit a high place in the road – probably a large rock – with the end of the tailpipe. That forced the entire tailpipe forward, folding the muffler up like a cheap tin can and shattering the catalytic converter.

They fixed things up. I would have to come back for a new catalytic converter – they did not have an extra one lying around their shop – but the car no longer sounded like I was headed to Bike Week at the beach, and off I went.

I decided I was not ready to go home and face other problems. The damaged car wasn't the only difficulty in my life; there were others, the same ones that many people struggle with. Along with those problems, and with the amount of money I laid out at the car place, I was preoccupied with how few birds I had seen that morning. The birdlessness of the morning had been eerie and had shaken me up more than the impact of the car hitting the rock.

I stopped at a modest city park to gather my wits. This little park was a far cry from the expansive forest I had been in that morning. It was the kind of place with a baseball field where the field is more weeds than grass, and where the trash cans are overflowing with wrappers from Taco Bell and empty plastic bottles of Michelob Light. Some languorous teenagers were sitting on the ground, immersed in their own world.

I took my binoculars and I walked up a grassy slope toward a bank of large, west-facing trees. The sun, dropping into the Taconic Mountains over my shoulder, illuminated the trees. The lower the sun dropped, the more the forest lit up. I staggered up the hill, thinking about the day's absence of birds, about my troubles, about the cost of catalytic converters. The metaphor of the setting sun was weighing on me.

Then it happened. In the outer branches of the trees that I was walking toward, lit up by the setting sun, I became aware of birds. And more birds and more birds. Then, all of them feeding actively on the edge of the forest, there were migrating birds everywhere.

Here's my eBird list from that late afternoon in that little urban park:

Springside Park, Berkshire, Massachusetts, US
Sep 12, 2016 5:45 PM– 7:26 PM
Protocol: Traveling, 1.45 mile(s)
Duration: 1 hour, 41 minutes

Mourning dove 2
Red-bellied woodpecker 4
Downy woodpecker 2
Hairy woodpecker 1
Northern flicker 4
Least flycatcher 1
Empidonax sp. 3
Eastern phoebe 6
Great crested flycatcher 1
Blue-headed vireo 2
Philadelphia vireo 1

Warbling vireo 2
Red-eyed vireo 2
Blue jay 12
American crow 4
Common raven 2
Black-capped chickadee 8
Tufted titmouse 6
White-breasted nuthatch 3
House wren (northern) 2
Gray catbird 5
Eastern bluebird 7
Veery 1
Swainson's thrush (olive-backed) 1
American robin 7
Cedar waxwing 3
Purple finch 1
American goldfinch 2
Chipping sparrow 3
Field sparrow 1
Song sparrow 4
Ovenbird 2
Black-and-white warbler 2
Tennessee warbler 1
Nashville warbler 1
Common yellowthroat 3
American redstart 7
Cape May warbler 1
Northern parula 3
Magnolia warbler 2
Bay-breasted warbler 2
Blackburnian warbler 2
Chestnut-sided warbler 3
Black-throated blue warbler 1
Pine warbler 1
Yellow-rumped warbler (Myrtle) 7
Black-throated green warbler 1

Canada warbler 1
Scarlet tanager 1
Rose-breasted grosbeak 2

Checklist comments: Most birds seen while I was stand-
ing in one spot in the meadow near the chestnut tree farm.
The bank of trees on the east side of the meadow was lit up
by the low sun in the west; the birds were moving steadily
through the trees, south to north. One of the greatest birding
experiences I've ever had.

I stood there stupefied, practically panting. In four decades of
birding, on multiple continents, I'd never seen anything quite like
this. I was watching forty-some species of migrating birds without
moving one step from my spot. It was like being in a birding video
game; or better, like watching a theatrical performance based on
migrating birds, with a soundtrack by Brahms or Monk. All these
little birds, pouring south, to the southern United States and the
Caribbean and Central America and South America – right here
in this little modest city park in Massachusetts. All of them, filled
with the courage it would take to get them there. My heart was
pounding. I kept reflexively wiping the lenses of my binoculars,
as if they weren't working right.

Since then, I've learned there's an explanation for what I wit-
nessed that afternoon. Insects, as the sun sets, move instinctively in
the direction of the setting sun, in hopes of extending the warmth
and productivity of the day. And the birds follow those insects.
What I was seeing was that all the insects, and all the birds, had
travelled as far as they could before coming to an insurmountable
obstacle – the big meadow I was standing in, which they didn't
want to cross. For the purposes of their day, they had come to the
end of the line.

For me too, because at this point, I was really late to get home.
I went back to the car and drove away, the sun falling behind the
mountains.

Hours later I was in bed and I closed my eyes. The birds were in the trees. The kids in the park hollered. I might have been thinking about population dynamics or ecological collapse or the astonishing cost of replacement catalytic converters, but I was thinking about Mary Oliver: *Tell me, what is it you plan to do with your one wild and precious life?* I had looked into the eye of the hurricane of bird migration. Everything around me, birds and bird migration and everything that drives it and everything else – I felt so tiny within it. Little and insignificant and wonderful. Everything was back in perspective. Meaning – that thing we strive for, but so easily and quickly lose our grip on – was back in the field of view.

Before the Sun Returns

Rosemerry Wahtola Trommer

On this gray morning,
I want to give you
the yellow of the oriole,
the way it weaves through
the invisible weight of the air.
So much touches us
we cannot see,
and we wonder why
we feel heavy.
I would give you, too,
the gray whir of the wings
of the hummingbird,
their improbable accuracy
as they negotiate the world
in search of what is sweet,
and I would give you joy
your own fine feet,
still learning to master
this art of moving
across the world
one step at a time,
this art of living into the pause
between footsteps –
that moment when
the body lifts
as if we, too, could fly.

Juncos
Curt Meine

Not to diss you other winter birds,
you red regal cardinals and blue cheeky jays,
industrious nuthatches and chirpy titmice,
lofty bald eagles and pert chickadees,
busy tree sparrows and roadside buntings,
woodpeckers checking your stations,
barred owls sounding your nighttime hours.
All good, and gratitude hereby given.

But you, all you gangs of *Junco hyemalis*,
charcoal hoods above prim white bellies,
rousting about from feeders to hillside,
bright beaks and eye beads leading the way,
enjoying your southern off-season, balmy
below the boreal, you sub-zero snowbirds,
I depend on you for your jolt of life in the
dead gray depths of the Wisconsin winter.

WESTERN TANAGER

Richard J. Nevle & Steven Nightingale

In German the word *zugunruhe* means a migratory restlessness, an anxious need to get up and move – and if you're a bird, to beat your wings and fly. *Zugunruhe* is a desire and a longing, a need, a biological imperative, a pull on the body by an invisible force. Consider the effect of this force on a small flame of a songbird – the western tanager. The bird is a seasonal migrant to the Sierra, who when compelled, perhaps by some reason of lengthening day or changing angle of sun, lofts its small, feathered body up into the sky from its wintering home among the altitudinous pine-oak woodlands of Mexico and Central America and heads northward. The bird travels by night, variably alone or in pairs or small flocks, navigating by starlight through high, rarefied air, journeying north through dark skies in an annual pilgrimage of more than a thousand miles to the forested heart of the Sierra Nevada.

Upon arrival, the birds claim their territory, announcing their presence with burry, robin-like songs called out from branches in the Sierra's conifer forests. They sing with questioning phrases – *cher'-we?, chee'-we?, chir'ru?, zee'-wer?* – from shady perches, hidden among the needles of tall conifers. The tanagers are surreptitious birds, more easily heard than seen, moving gently and deliberately, almost shyly among the limbs of trees. Many have described the tanager's behavior as subdued, even sluggish. Yet one cannot help but wonder if this just might be a learned wariness of being too beautiful.

When tanagers are spotted among the dun umbers and greens of the Sierra's conifer forest, it as though Christmastime suddenly and miraculously arrived in the midst of summer, decorating the pines and firs with feathered ornaments. The male tanagers' bright coloring, especially that of their summer breeding plumage, is quite the opposite of camouflage. Their bodies and wings are boldly patterned with black, white, and a luminous canary yellow. Their faces are dipped in an incandescent blush of red-orange, which the birds acquire from rhodoxanthin – a pigment possibly obtained from their meals of insects, who themselves extract the compound from meals of conifer needles. The male tanagers may be advertising brilliance in their prowess of the hunt – and their ability to provide for nestlings to come. Or perhaps they have evolved such vivid patterns of color simply because female western tanagers find it irresistibly sexy. Though we might swoon on seeing such a concentration of beauty distilled in this bright, feathered package of a bird, such vibrancy might too easily garner unwanted attention from sharp-eyed raptors of the forest – Cooper's or sharp-shinned hawks – who would just as soon devour the birds for a late lunch.

✳

The tanagers come to the Sierra to take sustenance from the bursts of abundant insect life and berries that arrive in late summer – and from this sustenance nurture their young. The female western tanager makes her nest – a small, loose cup of twigs woven with soft roots and grass and hair – high up in the branches of a conifer. She lays perhaps four eggs, each about the size of a small grape, each a pale hue of turquoise and decorated with a ring of umber splotches at the egg's blunt end. The parents feed their young with insects gleaned from bark or branches or snatched adroitly from the air while on the wing – even dragonflies, which they will soften up in their capable beaks before feeding them, head first, to their gaping-mouthed babies.

Yet danger lurks everywhere for the nestlings – from the predations of Steller's jays and nutcrackers; from owls and snakes and even bears; and too from female cowbirds. While tanagers are out foraging, this so-called nest parasite will seize upon the parents' momentary absence and in secret she will lay a speckled egg among the unhatched brood. Some days later, a cowbird nestling will take eagerly from the tanagers' offerings, freeloading on their provisions of food and child rearing services intended for their own.

✳

Come late summer, the green of Sierra meadows fades to dun, and nights again turn chill. The mountains exhale. Life gradually and gently subsides to the foothills, to the Great Basin, to the burrow underground, to the shelter of a tree-bark crevice, to the tropical woodland half a world away. With shortening days the western tanager's compass turns south. The male's facial flush fades to just an ember of scarlet flame, and his canary-colored feathers dull to an almost oliveish yellow. Male and female of the species merge closer in appearance. Parents depart on the wing. The summer-fledged young will follow a few weeks later, pulled by the mysterious force of *zugunruhe* for the first time. The tanagers take refuge in the deserts of the southwest, where they refuel, molt, and refresh their plumage before continuing on to wintering grounds of the high tropical woodlands of oak and pine, still a thousand miles farther south. Each western tanager may make the annual journey to the Sierra Nevada and back again to its wintering grounds perhaps eight times during the course of its fleeting life. What passes beneath the tanager as it migrates across starlit skies? Iron palisades that will never impede it, steel cages that will never imprison its young, barbed-wire stockades that will never fence it in.

Might we dare to imagine such migration, such freedom of movement for ourselves, for all our wild and human family? Do we not all need to find a safe home where we can thrive? Are we not, each in our own time, possessed by an aching *zugunruhe* ? Does the universe not pull on each of us with a tug as familiar as thirst, as common as blood, as old as stars and stone and endless breath of Sierra sky?

Richard J. Nevle

❋

How do we name the joy that rises within us when we see a western tanager? It makes the mind sparkle, as if fireworks were about to be kindled there. The crimson head, the gilt oracular breast, the dark wings flecked with gold, their beautiful morning song, both peaceable and urgent: we see them and wonder how we might have such luck, as to be just there, just then, with her.

Richard writes of *zugunruhe* , the restless longing to move, to explore, to follow the stars to new ground. And the natural question arises: what migration might we undertake that would answer to our innermost need, our most clear calling, our shy and secret hopefulness? What is it that any of us hope for if not to make of our time on earth a source of life for those we love and for others – friends, strangers, and those we will never meet, even though our fates are woven together.

Part of the answer is a longing for place – for the Sierra, for a certain cabin in a river canyon, for a hardscrabble desert where we may see a cougar walking with effortless magnificence; for a mountain meadow where we might hear a tanager finish with a song its journey of a thousand miles. What can this one bird teach us? She breeds in the Sierra Nevada, and north to western

Canada; and even as far south as the Four Corners in the American southwest. And then in winter, flies down to Mexico, and to Costa Rica, Honduras, El Salvador, all in tropical Central America. We share with her this world. We have, like her, the chance to know both the temperate and the tropical forest. We have our own way of singing, of nesting, of caring for our young. Learning about her, we see the resemblance between us, the resonant affinity, the way we both need to make summer in the Sierra into a heartfelt homeland. And suddenly we know the migration, the interior movement, the longing that counts for us: it is the longing to yield ourselves, to lose ourselves in communion. It is our soul-deep, light-led need to see that we are not superior, not rulers, nor are we special, neither as a species nor as our separate selves. Instead we need the communion that is a beautiful undoing of our separate lives in favor of a blessed, wider, destined unity with the earth. Each of us must take on the work recommended to us by the twelfth-century poet Hakim Sanai: "unself yourself." The Sufis talk of *fana*: annihilation in the light of God. In the re-composition of ourselves after so ardent and necessary a vanishing, we have a chance to fly with the tanager, a chance for reverential adventure with life everywhere, whatever its form.

O falcon!
My fingertips
    On your wings —

Cougar, at last
In the afternoon,
    We nap together.

Hornets, may I
Wear your nest
    As a turban?

Coyotes, count
Me in. We'll caper
    Through debutante balls.

Bobcat, trust me
I pray, to babysit
    The kittens.

Bat, take me
With you for
    Psychedelic acrobatics.

Dragonfly, those
Colors – are you
    Professor of opals?

Moth, your wings
Unlock every one of
    The doors of midnight.

Water ouzel: gray,
Small, plain, shy,
    Packed with gods.

Owl: fierce,
Vigilant, predatory –
    It's about joy.

Meadowlark: without
Your song, spring would
    Stay home and sulk.

Hummingbird:
Sewing together the mind
    We need.

Steven Nightingale

Redwing Blackbirds: A Letter for Your Kindness
David Taylor

Redwing blackbirds perch sideways
    on the brown phragmites,
      growing on the edge of the pond.
In the evening,
only their red shoulders flash bright in the dimming light,
    the rustle of waves and sunset orange lavender,
against the oddity
    of watching people and wing unfold by the pond and
    sidewalks
trailing the edges,
      a couple walking their groomed sheltie.
The beer at this bar is good, though, and I can take in the crim-
son flashes of bird
    wings from stalk to stalk,
and their calling and calling.
Here's my letter to you for listening to me,
    there is cheer in unexpected color,
    of how blackbirds dart and rest on thin perches,
      the unconscious red shimmering in a way and
      a place, that
        I have to say,
I could not have imagined.

JOIN THE CHORUS:
A READER'S GUIDE TO
DAWN SONGS

Every spring
I hear the thrush singing
in the glowing woods
he is only passing through.
His voice is deep,
then he lifts it until it seems
to fall from the sky.
I am thrilled.
                        I am grateful.

— FROM IN OUR WOODS, SOMETIMES RARE MUSIC
BY MARY OLIVER

The first to awaken begin to sing in the darkness. As the Earth turns – day breaking – other voices – bird voices – join in. The dawn chorus is declaration, is reverie, is a reason for us to rise and greet the morning with wonderment and joy. The dawn chorus is mystery – it eludes the whys and wherefores of science. The dawn chorus invites apprenticeship to awe.

Dawn songs are unique to species. The completeness of the choir – no two performances ever the same – is seasonal. Many of the songsters are longitudinal migrants – they traverse vast landscapes and seascapes, travelling a North-South axis, seasonally. They court, breed, and raise their young in the northernmost reaches of their range – all places they must come to know intimately, then depart. Neotropical migrants are the greatest travelled of these birds – navigating by the sun, stars, visual landmarks, sounds, smells, wind patterns, and magnetic fields – on wings and prayers – between the breeding rounds in North America and the tropical regions of Mexico, Central America, and South America – south of the Tropic of Cancer. There are also latitudinal migrants who move between East-West reaches, altitudinal migrants who breed on high then move downslope to counter food limitations and harsh weather conditions, and nomads who don't have fixed patterns but do as they must to survive seasonal shortcomings. We celebrate them, all.

Bird migration is motivated and informed by ancient rhythms. The history of birds is inexplicably tied to the history of planetary processes. The future of birds is explicitly tied to our humanity – the choices we make as *Homo sapiens* – inclusive or exclusive of each other and other species. We regard every *other thing* as part of a whole – a system of vibrant, vibrating life force on the move with something unique to say into the void of creation. We believe in the potential and power of songs aroused – arising – from the human heart as the light creeps in.

What is your uplifted song? How do you move through the world? This Reader's Guide is an invitation to explore this collection of works at the interface of Nature and human nature. We offer questions and activities to enable you to trek inner and outer landscapes from new perspectives. Let the words be callings: relational calls, flight calls, alarm calls, begging calls. Hear the authors' songs, as well as their chip notes, cries, screes, quacks, honks, hoots, and tremolos.

Want to help amplify *Dawn Songs?* Want to help *Dawn Songs* travel far and wide? Use the Reader's Guide to seed gatherings and conversations – bird clubs and book clubs, outdoor education programs, environmental festivals, remarks from the pulpit and podium and podcast and pond edge. We thank you for showing up in this way, wherever you are, with whatever you have to say as the darkness fades away.

QUESTIONS & ACTIVITIES

We invite you to express your answers through the literary, visual, musical, or performance arts – and to garner the courageous vulnerability to have them witnessed. Grip the perch. Sing it out.

To Know

1. Understanding the nature of a bird requires attentiveness and devotion – unyielding curiosity, long observant hours in the field despite the weather conditions, learning from other people's observations, finding answers and generating more questions to pursue. How do the authors in this section come to know of birds and bird migration? In what ways do they come to know themselves better? What are your own experiences in this regard? How has attentiveness to birds, or other wild flora and fauna, made you a more insightful person? How have birds made you a better person? Do something for the birds as an act of gratitude.

2. Do the authors in this section come to know landscapes through birds or birds through landscapes? What does this "knowing" require of the author? What does it require of the bird? What does it require of the place? Consider the place you reside and the migratory birds that also know this place for part of the year. How do you become knowledgeable about these birds? In what ways do they demonstrate knowledge of you? Imagine what the *Migratory Bird Field Guide to Humans* would include and convey! Go ahead, put it out there.

3. In what way does "not knowing" influence the authors in this section? What emotions and actions does it invoke? How might "the unknown" inspire you to learn more about birds, about Nature, about yourself? Make a list of the personal lessons the authors learned in the process of birding their way from the unknown to the knowable. Live into that list.

To Wonder

1. Despite advances in science and technology, there remains much to be learned about birds – and of ourselves. Knowledge of the miraculous nature of life can induce wonderment when it strikes the chord of humility. Wonderment can also be induced in the absence of knowledge – in mystery, awe, and astonishment. What do the authors in this section wonder about and how do the birds invoke this sense of wonderment? Are the wonderings big or small? Do they have personal or transpersonal consequence? What space does wonderment occupy in your life? In what ways have birds been a source of wonder for you, for your family, for your community? How could bird watching, or other ways of being nature-attentive, provide an opportunity for an even more wondrous life? Grab the binoculars and find out.

2. As we humans sleep, streams of migratory birds ply the starry skies over our dreamscapes. In their journeys, some short and others measured in thousands of miles over oceans and continents, they stitch the world together with wings. They speak to one another in transit with chips and secret languages we'll likely never know. We can only wonder what a migrating bird must see, feel, and think. When they land to rest, to refuel – or perhaps arrive at a "final" destination to breed, nest, winter or simply be – notes emerge. Have you ever wondered what it would it might be like to be one of these birds? What would your notes sound like? What would be the nature of their

meaning? Who do you hope awakens, hearing your voice? Categorize each "song" in this section by call type (using scientific terms and/or ones of your own making). What is the message the author conveys? Who do they hope to awaken?

3. In bird conservation, what is the value of mystery? How do the authors in this section speak to that value? How can you act on that value in your life? Consider how you can use mystery to strengthen bird conservation in your community. Then, step into the mystery.

To Lament

1. Lament is typically regarded as a passionate expression of grief, of sorrow, of regret, of loss – as an act of mourning something or someone. When we lament – bemoan, bewail, deplore – we are announcing that something has mattered to us. We have recognized a value is something beyond ourselves. Secretly perhaps, we are also crying out for vision to guide us across the thresholds of what was, through the ideals of what could have been, to the possibilities that have yet to arise. What are the authors in this section lamenting? What do they value? What varying roles have birds played in their lamenting process? What visions are they calling upon for birds, for themselves, for humanity? Which of their stories resonate with your own – in what way, specifically? Are their laments that you have yet to express? Find a way for the birds to help you do so.

2. Why might migratory birds serve as such as strong invocator for the lamenting process? There are pieces lamenting something to do with birds and to pieces lamenting something to do with people. In what ways are they similar? In what ways are they different? Determine what migratory bird best represents your laments and give the bird an opportunity to express them, dramatically.

3. In what ways do the authors' laments take them to a better place – literally, figuratively, mythologically? Consider how you can leverage lament for self-betterment, humanity-betterment, conservation-betterment. Do it.

To Celebrate

1. Celebration can be loud and boastful. Celebration can be quiet and reflective. It can be planned or spontaneous. What are the authors in this section celebrating and how do they celebrate? What various roles do birds play in the celebratory invocation or act? Conservation messaging is often framed from a problem-oriented perspective – at the extremes, doomsaying, blaming, and shaming. What role does celebration play in motivating and empowering conservation? What role could it play? How do you celebrate birds? How could you engage in even more celebratory actions? How could your acts of celebration – your joy – invite others to flock alongside you, to sing alongside you? Gather. Sing. Find out.
2. For the authors in this section, what circumstances invoke a sense of celebration? What were the birds doing? What were the bird watchers doing? At the interface of the two, what happened – specifically – to make a particular moment celebratory? Have you ever had a similar moment? If not, what has stopped you? Consider what you can do for yourself – and others – to foster celebratory events that are of and for the birds. Then, go enjoy!
3. Birds have long been symbols for human expression – in mythology, in craft, in art. Each of the *Dawn Songs* authors in this section share a story about a particular species that has invoked a sense of celebration. What do these species have in common? In what ways are they surprisingly different? From your perspective, what migratory bird best represents joy? Why this particular bird? Find a way to spread this bird-joy to others.

To Integrate

1. Across the collection there are bird species that show themselves multiple times – bank swallows, great blue herons, ruby-throated hummingbirds, snowy owls, and western tanagers, for example. How are the authors' "songs" of these species similar or different? Why? What makes for a particular "birding" experience? How much of the sense of the experience is about the bird and how much about the bird watcher? Gather a group of friends or colleagues and ask them to share their experiences, thoughts, and sentiments about a specific species of bird. How far and deeply has that bird alighted in human story?

2. Bird migration takes various twists and turns throughout the collection. What did you learn from a scientific perspective? What did you feel from a human perspective? What questions arose – like: What is home to a migratory bird? What have been your "migratory" patterns? In what way have these journeys – outer and inner – been related to the need to follow resources and/or move away from harsh conditions? What did your ancestors know of longitudinal, lateral, and altitudinal changes in geography? What insights can bird migration – as science and as mythos – offer regarding the nature of human dis-placement? Tell your story as if it is the story of a migrating bird.

3. Each of the *Dawn Songs* authors orients to a different geographic range – the bird's and their own. What does your personal range map look like? What limits or expands your range? What are the societal implications of small versus large "human ranges?" Bird watching can help you expand your range – literally and figuratively. What are you waiting for? Adventures – and perhaps big, juicy, green caterpillars – await.

Attributions & Notes

Buckley, BJ. Unbearable lightness. For J. Drew Lanham.

Clifford, Maggie. Wait for dawn. Lyrics inspired by Jamie K. Reaser's poem, Come back to me (this volume).

Coulter, Hope. Mississippi kite, late summer. Italicized excerpts from Lloyd Stone's "This Is My Song."

Faerstein, Howie. To the wary fox sparrow rustling in the leaf litter. Previously published in *Nine Mile Magazine* & Faerstein, Howie. 2018. *Googootz and Other Poems*, Press 53, LLC: Winston-Salem, North Carolina.

Griffin, Shaun T. Red-headed woodpecker. For Craig and Dez.

Lanham, J. Drew. Merlin medicine. Previously published in Lanham, J. Drew. 2020. *Sparrow Envy: A Guide to Birds and Lesser Beasts*. Hub City Press: Spartansburg, South Carolina.

Lanham, J. Drew. Migration. Previously published in Lanham, J. Drew. 2020. *Sparrow Envy: A Guide to Birds and Lesser Beasts*. Hub City Press: Spartansburg, South Carolina.

Lanham, J. Drew. Nocturne. Previously published in Lanham, J. Drew. 2020. *Sparrow Envy: A Guide to Birds and Lesser Beasts*. Hub City Press: Spartansburg, South Carolina.

Lanham, J. Drew. Prairie dreams. Previously published in Lanham, J. Drew. 2020. *Sparrow Envy: A Guide to Birds and Lesser Beasts*. Hub City Press: Spartansburg, South Carolina.

Lanham, J. Drew. Thrush love. Previously published in Lanham, J. Drew. 2020. *Sparrow Envy: A Guide to Birds and Lesser Beasts*. Hub City Press: Spartansburg, South Carolina.

Lanham, J. Drew. Zugunruhe on canvas. This piece is an exercise in ekphrastic feather praise inspired by Charley Harper's painting, Mystery of the Missing Migrants.

Levoy, Deborah. Blue heron. Lyrics inspired by lines in Pileated Woodpecker *Dryocopus pileatus* by Steven Nightingale as published in Nevle, Richard J. and Nightingale, Steven. 2022. *The Paradise Notebooks: 90 Miles Across the Sierra Nevada*. A Comstock Publishing Associates book published by Cornell University Press: Ithaca, New York.

Meine, Curt. Bird watching. For George and Charlie.

Moore, Kathleen Dean. Common murre. Excerpt from Moore, Kathleen Dean. 2021. *Earth's Wild Music: Celebrating and Defending the Songs of the Natural World*. Counterpoint Press: Berkeley, California.

Moore, Kathleen Dean. Dawn chorus. Excerpt from Moore, Kathleen Dean. 2021. *Earth's Wild Music: Celebrating and Defending the Songs of the Natural World*. Counterpoint Press: Berkeley, California.

Moore, Kathleen Dean. Swallows, falling. This piece was written to be accompanied by Sibelius Impromptu No. 5 in B minor Op. 5.

Morgan, Gwendolyn. Robins, runes, ospreys. Previously published in Morgan, Gwendolyn. 2016. *Snowy Owls, Egrets & Unexpected Graces*. Homebound Publications: Pawcatuck, Connecticut. Reprinted with permission of the author and publisher. The quote included is from Coyhis, D.L. 2007. *Meditations with Native American Elders: The Four Seasons, Hopi*. Coyhis Publishing & Consulting: Colorado, Colorado Springs.

Nevle, Richard K. The visitor. Adapted from the talk, *Natural History is a Compass that Points to Love: Lessons from a Falcon, a Warbler, and a Yosemite Ranger*, given as part of the 2020 Parsons Memorial Lodge Speaker Series in Yosemite National Park.

Nevle, Richard J. and Nightingale, Steven. Western tanager. Excerpt from Nevle, Richard J. and Nightingale, Steven. 2022. *The Paradise Notebooks: 90 Miles Across the Sierra Nevada*. A Comstock Publishing Associates book published by Cornell University Press: Ithaca, New York. Reprinted by permission of the publisher.

Patterson, Jr., Steve A. Swallow flight. Previously published in the *Trestle Creek Review.*

Reaser, Jamie K. The ovenbird (What to learn). Previously published in Reaser, Jamie K. 2019. *RidgeLines: A View of Nature and Human Nature.* Talking Waters Press: Stanardsville, Virginia.

Reaser, Jamie K. In the woods. Previously published in Reaser, Jamie K. 2019. *Conversations with Mary: Words of Attention and Devotion.* Talking Waters Press: Stanardsville, Virginia.

Root, William Pitt. Artic. For Robert Hedin. Previously published in Root, William Pitt. 1981. *Reasons for Going It on Foot.* Atheneum: New York.

Root, William Pitt. Wheel turning on the hub of the sun. Previously published in Root, William Pitt. 1981. *Reasons for Going It on Foot.* Atheneum: New York.

Root, William Pitt. Query for owl at spring equinox. Previously published in Root, William Pitt. 2013. *Strange Angels: New Poems.* Wings Press: San Antonio, Texas.

Schnuelle, Kim. Mandorla (Fall crossing). The facing pages of this poem are intended for two voices. The final stanza, right-aligned, is to be read in unison.

Sheffield, Derek. Bye-bye. Previously published in Sheffield, Derek. 2013. *Through the Second Skin.* Orchises Press: Alexandria, Virginia.

Sheffield, Derek. Living on James Wright. Previously published in Sheffield, Derek. 2013. *Through the Second Skin.* Orchises Press: Alexandria, Virginia.

Sheffield, Derek. Wilson's warbler. Appeared in *The Massachusetts Review.*

Uschuk, Pamela. Hummingbird. Previously published in Uschuk, Pamela. 1990. *Without Birds, Without Flowers, Without Trees.* Flume Press (Chapbook Award): Chico, California & Uschuk, Pamela. 2005. *Scattered* Risks. Wings Press: Chicago, Illinois.

Uschuk, Pamela. Snow goose migration at Tule Lake. Previously published in Uschuk, Pamela. 1990. *Without Birds, Without Flowers, Without Trees.* Flume Press (Chapbook Award): Chico, California & Uschuk, Pamela. 2005. *Scattered Risks.* Wings Press: Chicago, Illinois.

Uschuk, Pamela. Western tanager. Previously published in Uschuk, Pamela. 2022. *Refugee.* Red Hen Press: Los Angeles, California.

Wade, Sidney. Loons. Previously published in Wade, Sidney. 2017. *Bird Book: Poems.* Atelier26 Books: Portland, Oregon.

Acknowledgments

It was passed from one bird to another,
the whole gift of the day.
The day went from flute to flute,
went dressed in vegetation,
in flights which opened a tunnel
through the wind would pass
to where birds were breaking open
the dense blue air –
and there, night came in.

— FROM BIRD BY PABLO NERUDA

Our deepest gratitude to Mark Collins for the cover art and Jason Kirkey for book layout and cover design. We appreciate Mark Collins and Ky Scott lending their keen eyes to the final round of proofreading. Thanks are also due to Richard Nevle and Sean Hill for calling out to colleagues to join in the *Dawn Songs*, and to Gunars Platais for editing Spanish to English translations with poetic flair. Most of all, we are grateful to the birds for showing up, time and time again.

About *Dawn Songs*

Dawn Songs: A Birdwatcher's Field Guide to the Poetics of Migration is more than a book. It is an invocation – a calling together of birds and bird watchers across diverse landscapes and indefinite identities. It is a celebration of what unites us at the edges of Nature and human nature. It is, in part, Emily Dickinson's "Hope [being] the thing with feathers."

Dawn Songs proceeds are donated to the American Bird Conservancy's (ABC) Conservation and Justice Fellowship program. Through scientific research, community engagement, and storytelling, Fellows explore the interconnectedness of bird conservation and environmental justice. Applications are actively sought from a diversity of people, including people historically without voice in environmental justice and conservation dialogues. To learn more or further support the program, please contact the American Bird Conservancy, Conservation and Justice Fellowship program, P.O. Box 249, The Plains, VA 20198 or visit ABC online: abcbirds.org.

Join us in the *Dawn Songs* call by creating opportunities for youth from communities not traditionally at home in the wondrous outdoors to go bird watching – to find a place in the other-than-human world that facilitates reflection, belonging, and collective trauma healing. As the birds flock, help us to call together – people to place, people to things with feathers, people to the kindred spirits found in each other.

About
International [World]
Migratory Bird Day

Most species of Neotropical migrants are, as yet, not endangered.
We have the opportunity to conserve species before
they reach the ecologically precarious, politically unpopular,
and economically demanding status of endangerment.

— FROM THE HAND THAT ROCKS THE CRADLE,
GRASSROOTS MAGAZINE, BY JAMIE K. REASER

International Migratory Bird Day [IMBD] was founded by the
Smithsonian Migratory Bird Center in partnership with the Infor-
mation and Education Working Group of the Partners in Flight-
Aves de las Americas Program. The National Fish and Wildlife
Foundation played a key supporting role through Partners in Flight
operations.

Initially celebrated on May 8, 1993, IMBD was the first hemi-
sphere-wide, grassroots effort to educate and empower concerned
citizens on Neotropical migratory bird conservation. It provided
a platform for conservation efforts already underway throughout
the Western Hemisphere and inspired others into action. Federal
officials, lobbyists, and bird enthusiasts of all ages and walks of
life worked together toward a common goal – the celebration of
birds that transverse the Americas. The concern of scientists was
taken to the media, the public, and legislators. Event organizers
in North America joined forces with their counterparts in Latin
America. Children, as well as adults, learned to "see" and care for
migrants for the very first time.

In 2007, IMBD coordination transferred to Environment for
the Americas (EFTA), a non-profit organization that strives to

connect people to bird conservation. In 2018, EFTA joined with the Convention on Migratory Species (CMS) and the Agreement on the Conservation on African-Eurasian Migratory Waterbirds (AEWA) to launch a single, global bird conservation education campaign. IMBD was expanded to become World Migratory Bird Day (WMBD). Bird migration is now celebrated on the second Saturday in May across the African-Eurasian flyway, the East Asian-Australasian flyway, and the Americas flyway with a single, unifying conservation theme and message.

Dawn Songs is a contribution to the 30th Anniversary of IMBD. May the celebration continue. May conservation succeed. May dawn be songful.

About the Editors

J. Drew Lanham, PhD, is an Alumni Distinguished Professor of Conservation and Cultural Ornithology at Clemson University. He is the author of *The Home Place: Memoirs of a Colored Man's Love Affair with Nature, Sparrow Envy*, and *Sparrow Envy: Field Guide to Birds and Lesser Beasts*. His work has been recognized with the Reed Award from the Southern Environmental Law Center and the Southern Book Prize. He was a finalist for the John Burroughs Medal. Most notably, he received the prestigious MacArthur Foundation Fellowship in 2022—an award that recognizes and supports creative genius. Drew is a regular contributor to Orion Magazine and a much sought-after speaker in ornithological and literary circles. He is the Poet Laureate of Edgefield, South Carolina.

Jamie K. Reaser, PhD, is the author of ten full-length poetry and lyrical prose collections, the editor of two prosaic anthologies, and co-author of *Bring Back the Birds: What You Can Do to Save Threatened Species*. She is the recipient of two Nautilus Book Awards. Jamie has been an avid birdwatcher since early childhood. Over the course of her career, she has translated that passion into roles as an ecologist, educator, international policy negotiator, artist, and regenerative farmer. Jamie is the co-founder of the Smithsonian Migratory Bird Center and International [World] Migratory Bird Day. She is tended by the Rockfish River in central Virginia.